Life *by* Design

James Allen (1864–1912) retired from the business world to pursue a lifestyle of writing and contemplation. His books are classics in the fields of inspiration and spirituality. Although this is his most popular work, he authored several other books that deal with the power of thought including *The Path of Prosperity*, *Eight Pillars of Prosperity* and *James Allen's Book of Meditation for Every Day in the Year*.

Life *by* Design

Building Your Ideal Life with
Purpose and **Power**

JAMES ALLEN

RUPA

Published by
Rupa Publications India Pvt. Ltd 2024
7/16, Ansari Road, Daryaganj
New Delhi 110002

Sales centres:
Bengaluru Chennai
Hyderabad Jaipur Kathmandu
Kolkata Mumbai Prayagraj

Edition copyright © Rupa Publications India Pvt. Ltd 2024

All rights reserved.
No part of this publication may be reproduced, transmitted, or stored in a retrieval system, in any form or by any means, electronic, mechanical, photocopying, recording or otherwise, without the prior permission of the publisher.

P-ISBN: 978-93-6156-652-3

First impression 2024

10 9 8 7 6 5 4 3 2 1

Printed in India

This book is sold subject to the condition that it shall not, by way of trade or otherwise, be lent, resold, hired out, or otherwise circulated, without the publisher's prior consent, in any form of binding or cover other than that in which it is published.

Contents

Introduction: The Blueprint of Life vii

Vision and Mindset

1. Visionary Architect–Crafting Your Life's Vision 3
2. Mindset Mastery–The Power of Positive Thinking 21
3. The Time Sculptor–Mastering Time Management 40

Daily Practices and Emotional Well-being

4. The Habit Builder–Constructing a Routine for Success 55
5. Emotional Engineer–Designing Emotional Resilience ... 73
6. Relationship Architect–Building Strong Connections 100

Practical Aspects of Life

7. Financial Designer–Crafting Financial Stability 125
8. Health Innovator–Creating a Balanced Lifestyle 156

Personal Growth and Creativity

9. The Creative Craftsman–Unleashing Your Creativity ... 195
10. The Knowledge Seeker–Continuous Learning and Growth 230

Introduction
The Blueprint of Life

Each individual is both the architect and builder of their own destiny. Life, with its intricate patterns and unforeseen turns, can seem daunting without a clear plan or direction. Imagine embarking on a journey without a map or constructing a building without blueprints; chaos would ensue. Similarly, to build an ideal life brimming with purpose and power, one must start with a solid blueprint. This blueprint is not merely a set of plans but a dynamic, evolving guide that adapts to our growing understanding of ourselves and our surroundings.

At the heart of this blueprint lies the understanding that life is not a series of random events but a purposeful journey. This journey requires us to set a strong foundation, embrace our inherent purpose, and embark with unwavering determination. Let's delve into the comprehensive, multifaceted approach to designing and living our ideal life.

Building an ideal life is akin to assembling IKEA furniture—challenging, occasionally frustrating, but ultimately rewarding (and with fewer leftover screws, hopefully). It demands dedication, resilience, and a clear sense of purpose. Make conscious choices, set and achieve goals, and keep your actions aligned with your values and vision.

Life is not merely a collection of random events; it is a

deliberate and purposeful journey, guided by our choices, values, and goals. Each moment, whether a triumph or a setback, serves as a stepping stone on this path, pushing us forward or offering lessons that shape the person we are becoming.

Every decision, big or small, creates a ripple effect that influences the direction of our lives. The seemingly insignificant choices accumulate over time, crafting the life we live. Even the obstacles we encounter aren't just random challenges; they are opportunities for growth, resilience, and transformation. These moments test our resolve, teaching us patience and fortitude, and often revealing new strengths we didn't know we possessed.

This journey is not linear, and it's rarely smooth. There are detours, surprises, and moments when the road ahead seems unclear. But even in those uncertain times, there is purpose. The unexpected twists and turns often lead us to places we hadn't considered, opening doors to possibilities we never imagined.

By approaching life with a sense of purpose, we transform it from a series of disconnected events into a meaningful narrative. Each chapter and each decision contributes to a larger story—one that is uniquely ours. So, rather than seeing life as a random series of occurrences, recognize it as a purposeful adventure, where every moment, every experience, is part of a grander design that leads you closer to your true self and the fulfillment of your deepest aspirations.

VISION AND MINDSET

1

Visionary Architect–Crafting Your Life's Vision

Designing your life is an ever-evolving journey that begins with self-awareness and is guided by core values, vision, and purpose.

It involves setting goals, building positive habits, and overcoming challenges with resilience and a good laugh. By following this extensive blueprint, you can build an ideal life that reflects your true self and brings lasting joy, satisfaction, and a few good stories to tell along the way.

Ultimately, our lives are the sum of our choices and actions. As we navigate the twists and turns, it is crucial to remain adaptable, learning from each experience and adjusting our course as needed. Every step, whether a leap forward or a cautious shuffle, contributes to the grand design of our existence. Cherish the moments of triumph, and find humor in the stumbles, for they are all part of the rich tapestry of life. With a clear blueprint in hand and an adventurous spirit, we can transform our aspirations into reality, crafting a life that is uniquely ours and profoundly meaningful.

Consider this: each sunrise is a blank canvas, and every decision we make is a brushstroke that shapes our destiny. We are the artists of our lives, blending colors of experiences, shading with shadows of challenges, and highlighting with moments of joy and success. The masterpiece we create is not just a reflection of our dreams but a testament to our resilience and creativity.

Embracing the unpredictability of life with a sense of curiosity and courage allows us to explore new horizons and uncover hidden potentials. Just as an architect envisions a magnificent structure from a mere sketch, we too can visualize and construct a life of purpose and power. By continuously refining our blueprint, we ensure that our journey is not only guided by intention but also enriched by the surprises and lessons that each new day brings.

In the grand scheme of life, we are both the dreamers and the doers, capable of shaping our future with the strength of our convictions and the flexibility to adapt. This duality empowers us to face the unknown with confidence, turning obstacles into opportunities and dreams into reality. So, take the leap, embrace the journey, and design a life that is not just lived but truly celebrated.

SETTING THE FOUNDATION FOR YOUR IDEAL LIFE

1. Self-Awareness: The Bedrock of Purpose

The cornerstone of building an ideal life is self-awareness. Without understanding who we are, our strengths, weaknesses, passions, and fears, we cannot begin to lay the first stone. This self-awareness comes from introspection and honest evaluation. Journaling, meditation, and feedback from trusted friends and mentors are invaluable tools in this process.

For example, consider the story of Maya, a successful corporate lawyer who felt unfulfilled despite her accomplishments.

Through deep self-reflection, she realized her true passion was in environmental law, advocating for sustainable practices. This epiphany led her to pivot her career, aligning her work with her values, and bringing her immense satisfaction.

Example: Tim's Artistic Awakening

Tim was an accountant. On the surface, his life seemed perfect: he had a stable job, a nice apartment, and a cat named Whiskers who only occasionally knocked things off the counter. Yet, Tim felt an inexplicable void. Through a combination of late-night journaling sessions and awkwardly deep conversations with Whiskers, he discovered that his true passion lay in painting murals.

Tim started small, painting in his garage and eventually taking on projects for friends. His breakthrough came when he was invited to paint a mural at a local community center. The joy and fulfillment he felt while painting were unlike anything he had experienced in his accounting career. Today, Tim is a renowned mural artist, spreading joy and color throughout his city.

2. Core Values: The Guiding Principles

Once self-awareness is achieved, the next step is identifying and solidifying core values. These values act as a compass, guiding decisions and actions. They define what is non-negotiable in our lives and ensure that we remain true to ourselves amidst external pressures.

Example: Sarah's Commitment to Sustainability

Sarah, a marketing executive, always felt a strong connection to nature. Growing up in a family that valued environmental conservation, she carried those values into her adult life.

However, her corporate job often clashed with her personal values, especially when she was asked to promote products that were not environmentally friendly.

After much reflection, Sarah decided to align her career with her values. She left her job and founded an eco-friendly marketing agency. Her agency focuses on promoting sustainable products and companies, and she has become a prominent voice in the green marketing world. By aligning her career with her core values, Sarah not only found professional success but also a deep sense of fulfillment.

3. Vision: The Blueprint of Aspiration

A clear, compelling vision of the future provides direction and motivation. This vision should be vivid and detailed, encompassing all aspects of life – personal, professional, social, and spiritual. It's not just about setting long-term goals but also about envisioning the daily life that supports those goals.

For instance, if someone's vision includes being a community leader, their daily actions must reflect leadership qualities, like integrity, empathy, and proactivity.

Example: Alex's Holistic Health Center

Alex was a personal trainer with a vision to create a holistic health center that combined fitness, nutrition, and mental well-being. His vision was detailed and specific: a center with state-of-the-art fitness equipment, organic juice bars, meditation rooms, and workshops on mental health and wellness.

Alex spent years refining his vision and setting actionable goals. He started by offering personal training sessions combined with nutrition advice. Gradually, he saved enough money and built a network of clients and experts who shared his vision. Today, Alex's holistic health center is a thriving hub where people come to transform their lives, embodying his vision of holistic well-being.

4. Goal Setting: The Milestones of Progress

Goals transform vision into actionable steps. They should be SMART (Specific, Measurable, Achievable, Relevant, Time-bound). Breaking down long-term aspirations into short-term, manageable tasks makes the journey less overwhelming and provides regular opportunities for accomplishment.

Example: Jenny's Academic Journey

Jenny, a high school teacher, dreamed of earning a PhD in educational psychology to better support her students. Her goal was specific: earn a PhD in five years. She broke this down into smaller, manageable tasks: researching programs, applying to schools, securing funding, and completing coursework and research.

Each semester, Jenny set specific goals for her studies and research. She balanced her job with her academic responsibilities, sometimes sacrificing weekends and evenings. Despite the challenges, Jenny stayed focused, and five years later, she proudly graduated with her PhD. Her accomplishment not only advanced her career but also enhanced her ability to support her students' psychological and educational needs.

5. Resilience: The Structural Integrity

Building an ideal life is not a smooth journey; setbacks and failures are inevitable. Resilience—the ability to bounce back and adapt – ensures that temporary failures do not derail the entire process. Developing a resilient mindset involves positive thinking, learning from failures, and maintaining a flexible approach to problem-solving.

Example: Tom's Entrepreneurial Resilience

Tom, a software developer, decided to launch his own tech startup. His initial product, a revolutionary app, was met with lukewarm reception and several technical issues. Investors pulled out, and Tom faced financial strain.

Instead of giving up, Tom embraced resilience. He analyzed feedback, made necessary adjustments, and pivoted his business model. He also sought mentorship and joined a startup accelerator program. After months of hard work, Tom's revamped app gained traction, and his startup started attracting investors and customers. Tom's journey taught him that resilience and adaptability are key to overcoming setbacks and achieving success.

EMBRACING THE POWER OF PURPOSE

1. The Essence of Purpose

Purpose is the driving force that fuels our journey. It's the deeper reason behind our actions and aspirations. Living with purpose means aligning daily actions with long-term goals and core values. It's about making choices that reflect our true selves and contribute to a greater good.

Example: Mia's Community Outreach

Mia, a social worker, always felt a strong calling to help her community. She realized that her purpose was to empower underprivileged youth. Mia launched a community outreach program offering mentorship, educational support, and recreational activities. Her program has transformed the lives of countless young people, providing them with opportunities and hope. Mia's deep sense of purpose drives her daily efforts and fuels her passion for making a difference.

2. Discovering Your Purpose

Discovering purpose is a profound and personal journey. It often involves looking beyond oneself to see how one's passions and skills can serve others. This can be achieved through volunteer work, mentorship, or engaging in activities that bring joy and fulfillment.

Example: David's Culinary Adventure

David, a corporate lawyer, felt unfulfilled despite his successful career. He took a sabbatical to explore his interests and discovered a passion for cooking. David enrolled in culinary school, volunteered at local food banks, and traveled to learn about different cuisines. Through these experiences, he realized that his purpose was to share his love of food with others.

David opened a restaurant that focuses on sustainable, farm-to-table dining. His culinary journey not only brought him personal fulfillment but also allowed him to contribute to his community by promoting sustainable practices and offering cooking classes.

3. Living with Purpose

Living with purpose requires consistent effort and reflection. It involves making conscious choices, prioritizing meaningful activities, and letting go of distractions that do not serve our higher goals. It also means being willing to make sacrifices and face challenges with determination and grace.

For instance, consider the life of Nelson Mandela, who endured years of imprisonment but remained steadfast in his purpose of ending apartheid. His unwavering commitment to his cause not only brought about significant social change but also inspired millions worldwide.

Example: Emma's Non-Profit Work

Emma, a marketing professional, discovered her purpose in animal welfare. She left her corporate job to work full-time for a non-profit organization dedicated to rescuing and rehabilitating abused animals. Emma's daily life is now filled with activities that reflect her values, from organizing fundraising events to coordinating rescue missions.

Living with purpose has brought Emma immense joy and fulfillment. She wakes up every day excited to make a difference, and her work has had a profound impact on countless animals and the community.

4. Purpose and Passion: The Dynamic Duo

Passion fuels purpose. It's the enthusiasm and energy that makes the journey enjoyable. When passion aligns with purpose, work feels less like a chore and more like a fulfilling endeavor. This powerful combination leads to sustained motivation and a sense of deep satisfaction.

Example: Carlos's Music Therapy

Carlos, a professional musician, found his purpose in helping others heal through music. He combined his passion for music with his desire to support mental health and became a certified music therapist. Carlos now works with individuals struggling with trauma, anxiety, and depression, using music as a therapeutic tool.

His sessions are filled with creativity, compassion, and healing. Carlos's passion for music and his purpose of helping others create a dynamic duo that brings joy and relief to his clients and immense satisfaction to his own life.

THE JOURNEY BEGINS: BUILDING WITH INTENTION AND ACTION

1. Taking the First Steps

Every grand journey begins with a single step. The first steps in building an ideal life are often the hardest, as they require breaking free from old habits and mindsets. It's essential to start small, focusing on achievable tasks that build momentum and confidence.

Example: Lily's Fitness Journey

Lily wanted to get fit but felt overwhelmed by the idea of intense workouts. She started small, committing to a 10-minute daily walk. Gradually, she increased the duration and intensity of her workouts. After a few months, Lily joined a local gym and began participating in fitness classes. Her incremental approach built her confidence and stamina, leading to significant improvements in her fitness level.

2. Creating a Daily Routine

A well-structured daily routine is a powerful tool for achieving long-term goals. It ensures that time is spent productively and that actions align with our vision and purpose. A balanced routine should include time for work, rest, exercise, and personal growth activities like reading, learning new skills, or meditation.

For example, successful individuals like Tim Ferriss emphasize the importance of a morning routine that sets a positive tone for the day. His routine includes activities like journaling, meditation, and physical exercise, which help him stay focused and energized.

Example: Tom's Writing Routine

Tom, an aspiring novelist, struggled to find time to write amidst his busy schedule. He decided to create a daily routine that included a dedicated hour for writing each morning. By waking up an hour earlier, Tom was able to write consistently without distractions. His routine also included time for exercise, reading, and relaxation, ensuring a balanced and productive day. Over time, Tom completed his first novel and began working on his second.

3. Building Positive Habits

Habits are the building blocks of our daily life. Positive habits, once ingrained, make it easier to maintain consistency and progress. It's crucial to identify and cultivate habits that support our goals and eliminate those that hinder our growth.

James Clear, in his book 'Atomic Habits,' illustrates how small, incremental changes in habits can lead to significant improvements over time. He emphasizes the power of 1% improvements and how they compound to create remarkable transformations.

Example: Laura's Financial Discipline

Laura wanted to improve her financial health and save for her dream home. She started by tracking her expenses and setting a budget. Laura developed positive habits like meal prepping to save on dining out, setting up automatic transfers to her savings account, and regularly reviewing her financial goals.

These habits helped Laura build financial discipline and steadily increase her savings. After a few years of consistent effort, she achieved her goal of buying her dream home.

4. Overcoming Obstacles

Challenges and obstacles are inevitable, but they are also opportunities for growth. Overcoming these obstacles requires a combination of perseverance, creativity, and support from others. It's important to view challenges as learning experiences and to seek solutions rather than dwell on problems.

Example: Jake's Academic Struggles

Jake, a college student, faced significant challenges in his engineering program. He struggled with advanced math courses and felt overwhelmed by the workload. Instead of giving up, Jake sought help from tutors, formed study groups, and used online resources to improve his understanding.

He also developed better time management skills and created a study schedule. Jake's persistence paid off, and he eventually excelled in his courses, graduating with honors and securing a job in his field.

5. Celebrating Progress

Recognizing and celebrating progress, no matter how small, is vital for maintaining motivation and momentum. It's important to acknowledge achievements, reflect on the journey, and express gratitude for the opportunities and lessons learned.

Example: Rachel's Language Learning

Rachel decided to learn Spanish to better communicate with her colleagues and clients. She set small, achievable goals like learning 10 new words each week and practicing with language apps. Rachel celebrated her progress by rewarding herself with small treats, like a favorite snack or a new book.

She also joined a local language exchange group, where she

practiced speaking Spanish with native speakers. Over time, Rachel's skills improved, and she felt confident enough to hold conversations in Spanish. Celebrating her progress kept her motivated and excited about learning.

To live a creative life, we must lose our fear of being wrong.

—Joseph Chilton Pearce

FINAL THOUGHTS: LIVING YOUR DESIGNED LIFE

Building your dream life is like putting together a complex LEGO set—challenging, sometimes exasperating, but incredibly satisfying when it all comes together. It takes commitment, persistence, and a clear direction. Make intentional decisions, set achievable milestones, and ensure your actions stay true to your values and long-term vision.

Remember, life isn't just a collection of random occurrences but a meaningful journey. Approach it with purpose, humor, and a bit of grace. By using this detailed, and occasionally amusing, roadmap, you can shape a life that is not only successful but also richly fulfilling and delightfully absurd in the best way possible.

To sum up, crafting your life is an ongoing adventure that starts with self-awareness, directed by your values, vision, and purpose. It means setting goals, developing good habits, and facing challenges with both resilience and a sense of humor. By following this thorough guide, you can create a life that truly represents who you are, bringing you lasting joy, satisfaction, and a few great stories to share.

In the meantime, there are a few DIY exercises for you to build yourself mentally strong.

STEP 1: SELF-AWARENESS BOOTCAMP

Task: The Mirror Monologue

Duration: 3 Days

Instructions:

1. Stand in front of a mirror for five minutes each morning and have a conversation with yourself. Address yourself by a ridiculous nickname (e.g., Captain Awesome or Baroness Brilliance).
2. Ask yourself questions like:
   - 'Captain Awesome, what hidden talents do you possess that the world has yet to discover?'
   - 'Baroness Brilliance, what fears are you secretly wrestling with?'
3. Record the highlights of these conversations in a journal titled 'Epic Self-Discoveries.'

Example:

On Day 1, Captain Awesome (you) realizes you have a knack for storytelling, which you've never explored. By Day 3, you admit to Baroness Brilliance that you fear public speaking, even though you've always wanted to perform stand-up comedy.

Reward:

Treat yourself to a 'Captain's Feast' (your favorite meal) at the end of the three days.

STEP 2: CORE VALUES SCAVENGER HUNT

Task: The Value Vault

Duration: 1 Week

Instructions:

1. List ten core values on individual slips of paper (e.g., honesty, creativity, adventure).
2. Hide these slips around your house or workplace in places that represent these values (e.g., creativity slip in your art supplies, honesty slip in your diary).
3. Each day, find one slip and write a short story about how this value has shaped your life. Share a funny anecdote related to each value.

Example:

On Day 2, you find the 'adventure' slip in your hiking boots. You write about the time you got lost on a hiking trail and ended up crashing a random family's picnic. You bonded over sandwiches and became lifelong friends.

Reward:

At the end of the week, host a 'Value Vault Party' with friends where you read your stories aloud, accompanied by value-themed snacks (e.g., 'Honesty Cookies' and 'Creativity Cocktails').

STEP 3: VISION QUEST

Task: The Vision Board Extravaganza

Duration: 2 Days

Visionary Architect–Crafting Your Life's Vision 17

Instructions:

1. Gather materials for a vision board: magazines, glue, scissors, markers, and a large poster board.
2. Spend the first day cutting out images and words that resonate with your ideal life. Include both serious aspirations (e.g., a dream job) and silly desires (e.g., owning a pet llama).
3. On the second day, assemble your vision board with a mix of humor and purpose. Create a section titled 'Totally Serious Goals' and another called 'Just for Giggles.'

Example:

Your 'Totally Serious Goals' section includes a picture of a bustling office where you imagine leading a creative team. The 'Just for Giggles' section features a llama in sunglasses with the caption, 'Future Llama Buddy.'

Reward:

Throw a 'Vision Board Reveal Party' with friends. Present your board in a dramatic fashion, complete with spotlights and applause sound effects.

STEP 4: GOAL SETTING RELAY RACE

Task: The Goal Gauntlet

Duration: 1 Week

Instructions:

1. Write down ten SMART goals (Specific, Measurable, Achievable, Relevant, Time-bound).
2. Assign each goal to a day of the week, leaving two days for relaxation and reflection.

3. Each day, focus on one goal and complete a mini-challenge related to it. Record your progress in a journal.

Example:

- **Monday:** Goal: 'Run a 5k without collapsing.' Mini-Challenge: Run/walk a mile and reward yourself with an extra-long bubble bath.
- **Wednesday:** Goal: 'Order a meal in French without accidentally asking for goat cheese in my coffee.' Mini-Challenge: Watch a French movie and practice ordering with subtitles.

Reward:

At the end of the week, award yourself a 'Goal Gauntlet Medal' (a DIY craft project) and wear it proudly around the house.

STEP 5: RESILIENCE OBSTACLE COURSE

Task: The Resilience Relay

Duration: 1 Week

Instructions:

1. Create a list of common obstacles you've faced (e.g., procrastination, fear of failure, distractions).
2. Each day, choose one obstacle and devise a fun and creative way to overcome it. Document your strategy and results.

Example:

Obstacle: Procrastination.

- **Strategy:** Create a 'Procrastination Penalty Box' where you have to sit and do nothing for 10 minutes if caught procrastinating.

- **Result:** You realize you'd rather do anything than sit in the penalty box, and you become more productive.

Reward:

Host a 'Resilience Awards Ceremony' where you give yourself awards like 'Procrastination Slayer' and 'Distraction Dodger.' Invite friends to join and share their own resilience stories.

STEP 6: CELEBRATION CARNIVAL

Task: The Victory Parade

Duration: 1 Day

Instructions:

1. Reflect on all the progress you've made throughout the treasure hunt. Gather all your journals, vision boards, and notes.
2. Organize a 'Victory Parade' in your living room. March around with your 'Goal Gauntlet Medal' and any other awards you've crafted. Play triumphant music and wave to your imaginary (or real) audience.
3. Share your journey with friends and family through a fun presentation or a social media post. Highlight both the serious achievements and the humorous moments.

Example:

Your Victory Parade includes a slideshow of your vision board, excerpts from your 'Epic Self-Discoveries' journal, and a reenactment of the time you had to sit in the 'Procrastination Penalty Box.'

Reward:

End the day with a 'Victory Feast' featuring your favorite foods, and toast to your newfound self-awareness, purpose, and resilience.

By completing this Life Design Treasure Hunt, you've not only created a comprehensive plan for building your ideal life but also had a blast doing it. Remember, the journey is just as important as the destination, especially when it's filled with laughter and creativity. Here's to a life designed with purpose, power, and a whole lot of fun!

2

Mindset Mastery—The Power of Positive Thinking

Design your life with intention, crafting each moment with purpose and power. For in the blueprint of your dreams lies the architecture of your destiny.

OVERCOMING LIMITING BELIEFS

Alright, let's dive headfirst into the carnival of the mind! Imagine your brain is a theme park, and in this park, you've got a bunch of rusty old rides called Limiting Beliefs. They creak, they groan, and worst of all, they keep you from enjoying the shiny new roller coasters of opportunity. Time to shut down those rusty rides and build something epic!

THE ULTIMATE GUIDE TO SPRUCING UP YOUR MENTAL GARAGE:

1. Identify the Rust Buckets:
- **Point:** Find those crusty old limiting beliefs hiding in the corners.
  - **Example:** 'I'll never be good at math' - Oh come on,

it's just numbers at a rave. Get your groove on!
- **Action:** Grab a pen and paper, hunt them down, and admit they're taking up space in your head.

▶ **Point:** Track down those mental clunkers.
- **Example:** 'I'm always late' - Really? Even a broken clock is right twice a day!
- **Action:** Jot them down like you're writing a confession for your mind's garage sale.

▶ **Point:** Pinpoint the self-doubt jalopies.
- **Example:** 'I can't cook' - Ever heard of ordering takeout? It's culinary magic.
- **Action:** List these doubts like you're making a grocery list of what NOT to buy.

2. Challenge the Oldies:

▶ **Point:** Put those outdated beliefs on trial.
- **Example:** 'Is it really true you can't speak in public? Remember when you rocked that karaoke night?'
- **Action:** Argue with yourself like you're Perry Mason. Present evidence that you're actually awesome!

▶ **Point:** Cross-examine those mental fossils.
- **Example:** 'Are you sure you can't dance? What about that time you did the Macarena perfectly?'
- **Action:** Turn into a mental detective and gather proof to dismantle those old convictions.

▶ **Point:** Scrutinize those ancient mental records.
- **Example:** 'Is it a fact that you're bad at sports? Remember that time you scored the winning goal in dodgeball?'
- **Action:** Have a courtroom-style showdown in your head, complete with gavel and dramatic objections.

3. Reframe and Rename:

▶ **Point:** Give those negative thoughts a makeover.

- **Example:** Change 'I'm terrible at starting conversations' to 'I'm discovering my inner chatterbox.'
- **Action:** Write your new belief on sticky notes and plaster them everywhere - mirrors, fridges, even your dog if they're cool with it.

▶ **Point:** Spin those downer thoughts into upbeat anthems.
- **Example:** Swap 'I'm bad with directions' for 'I'm exploring my adventurous spirit.'
- **Action:** Stick your new beliefs on anything that stands still long enough—laptops, lunchboxes, maybe even your shoes.

▶ **Point:** Transform gloomy thoughts into bright affirmations.
- **Example:** Turn 'I can't sing' into 'I'm finding my voice one note at a time.'
- **Action:** Make your new beliefs as visible as possible—on your desk, your car dashboard, and yes, even on your cat if they agree.

4. Act As If:

▶ **Point:** Live like you've already embraced the new belief.
- **Example:** Strut around like a peacock even if you feel like a pigeon.
- **Action:** Fake it till you make it. Keep practicing until your new belief feels like second nature.

▶ **Point:** Behave as if you're the superstar of your new mindset.
- **Example:** Walk with the confidence of a runway model even if you're in pajamas.
- **Action:** Role-play your new belief daily until it's as comfy as your favorite pair of jeans.

▶ **Point:** Pretend you're already the person you want to be.
- **Example:** Act like a gourmet chef even if you're just microwaving leftovers.

- **Action:** Keep at it with Oscar-worthy performances until your new belief becomes your reality.

Now, get out there and revamp your mental garage with style, sass, and a good dose of humor!

THE SCIENCE OF NEUROPLASTICITY AND MINDSET

Buckle up, science geeks and curious cats, we're diving into the brain's DIY workshop!

NEUROPLASTICITY: THE ULTIMATE BRAIN WORKOUT GUIDE

1. Neuroplasticity 101:
- **Point:** Think of your brain as a giant lump of Play-Doh, just waiting to be shaped and molded into something amazing!
  - **Example:** Imagine if London cab drivers can expand their hippocampus by memorizing every twist and turn of the city, surely you can stretch your brain muscles to achieve greatness. It's like turning your brain into a GPS system – how cool is that?
  - **Action:** Dive into new learning experiences with the enthusiasm of a kid let loose in a candy store. Whether it's picking up a new hobby, learning to juggle, or trying out those tricky Sudoku puzzles, embrace the process. Treat every new challenge like an adventure, and watch your brain grow stronger and more flexible.
- **Point:** Your brain is like a garden – nurture it and watch it flourish!
  - **Example:** If seasoned chefs can enhance their motor cortex through years of chopping, sautéing, and

flambéing, you can also cultivate your brain for brilliance. Picture your neurons donning tiny chef hats, busily working to perfect your mental recipes.
- **Action:** Approach new skills and experiences with the joy of a toddler discovering bubbles for the first time. Every time you learn something new, you're adding a fresh, vibrant flower to your brain's garden. So, go ahead and plant those seeds of knowledge and let your brain bloom!

▶ **Point:** Picture your brain as an artist's canvas, ready to be painted with the colors of knowledge.
- **Example:** Just like musicians fine-tune their auditory cortex by practicing scales and melodies, you too can tune your brain to your desired frequency. Think of your neurons as a symphony orchestra, each one playing its part in your cognitive masterpiece.
- **Action:** Jump into new learning opportunities with the excitement of opening a present. Whether it's learning to play the ukulele or mastering the art of origami, each new activity adds a unique brushstroke to your mental canvas. Get ready to create a brain that's a true work of art!

2. Building Better Pathways:
▶ **Point:** Picture your thoughts carving out neural pathways like a machete hacking through a dense jungle.
- **Example:** The more you tread the path of positivity, the more it becomes your brain's superhighway. Imagine forging a trail through the mental wilderness, each step making the route clearer and easier to follow.
- **Action:** Keep feeding your brain positive thoughts like a trail mix for the mind. Every time you choose optimism over doubt, you're paving a smoother path. Think of your

brain as a bustling highway construction site, constantly improving and expanding its positive routes.

- **Point:** Visualize your mind as a network of trails, each one becoming clearer with use.
  - **Example:** Just like a park ranger clears and maintains hiking paths, you can create well-worn trails of positivity in your brain. Imagine your thoughts wearing hiking boots, trekking through your mental forest.
  - **Action:** Reinforce positive thoughts until they become your brain's default trail. Think of it as sending your thoughts on a delightful hike every day, eventually transforming a rough path into a well-trodden route. Your mental park will soon be filled with beautiful, easy-to-navigate trails!
- **Point:** Envision your brain as a dynamic map with evolving routes.
  - **Example:** Just as a dedicated gardener tends to their plants, you can cultivate flourishing neural pathways. Imagine your thoughts as gardeners, carefully nurturing each neural connection.
  - **Action:** Continue to reinforce positive thoughts until they become the brain's preferred pathways. Think of it as sending your mental gardeners to work every day, transforming overgrown paths into lush, thriving pathways. Your brain will soon be a vibrant, well-maintained garden of positivity!

3. Use It or Lose It:

- **Point:** Remember, neurons that fire together, wire together—it's like a high-five for your brain cells!
  - **Example:** Treat your brain like a muscle that needs regular workouts. The more you use specific neurons, the stronger they get, just like biceps in a gym.

- **Action:** Engage in brain-challenging activities like learning a new language, playing a musical instrument, or tackling complex puzzles. Think of it as sending your neurons to brain boot camp, where they can flex their cognitive muscles and become brainy bodybuilders!
▶ **Point:** Imagine your brain as a bustling fitness center where neurons pump iron together.
  - **Example:** Just as a dedicated athlete builds strength through consistent training, you can strengthen your neural connections. Picture your neurons donning sweatbands and hitting the gym.
  - **Action:** Participate in activities that challenge your brain, such as learning to play chess, picking up knitting, or solving advanced logic puzzles. Treat it like an intense workout for your mind, ensuring your neurons stay in peak condition and ready for action.
▶ **Point:** Think of your brain as a sports team, where neurons practice together to perform at their best.
  - **Example:** Just like a basketball team improves through drills and scrimmages, your neurons enhance their connections through repeated use. Imagine your brain cells running drills and perfecting their plays.
  - **Action:** Take on activities that challenge your brain – whether it's mastering a new recipe, exploring a foreign language, or solving intricate riddles. Consider it a rigorous training session for your neurons, preparing them to excel in the cognitive championships.

4. Mindset Shifts:
▶ **Point:** Switch from a fixed mindset to a growth mindset and watch your brain blossom.
  - **Example:** Carol Dweck's research shows that believing in your ability to improve (growth mindset) leads to

actual improvement. Think of it as giving your brain a superhero cape – with the right mindset, anything is possible!
- **Action:** Embrace challenges, persist through setbacks, and view effort as a pathway to mastery. Treat every obstacle like a fun puzzle to solve, knowing that each attempt strengthens your brain's resilience and adaptability.

▶ **Point:** Transform your mental landscape from a barren desert to a thriving jungle with a growth mindset.
- **Example:** Carol Dweck's studies highlight that believing in your capacity for growth fosters real progress. Picture your brain as a fertile ground where new ideas and skills can sprout and flourish.
- **Action:** Welcome challenges, endure through difficulties, and see effort as the key to unlocking your potential. Approach each hurdle like an exciting adventure, knowing that every experience enriches your mental jungle with new growth and vitality.

▶ **Point:** Shift your perspective from a fixed mindset to a dynamic, ever-evolving one.
- **Example:** Carol Dweck's findings reveal that adopting a growth mindset leads to genuine improvement. Imagine your brain as a vibrant ecosystem, teeming with possibilities and growth.
- **Action:** Embrace challenges, persist through setbacks, and view effort as the route to mastery. Treat every difficulty like a thrilling quest, knowing that each step forward nurtures your brain's continuous evolution and expansion.

By expanding on each point with detailed and humorous

examples, we create an extensive, engaging, and entertaining guide to neuroplasticity, mindset shifts, and mental exercises. This approach not only provides valuable information but also makes the content enjoyable and easy to relate to.

> *The groundwork for all happiness is good health.*
>
> —Leigh Hunt

DAILY AFFIRMATIONS AND MENTAL EXERCISES

Welcome to the ultimate daily gym session for your mind!

Time to flex those mental muscles and get that positivity pumping!

1. Morning Mantra:
- **Point:** Kickstart your day with powerful affirmations.
  - **Example:** 'Today, I am capable of achieving anything I set my mind to.'
  - **Action:** Stand in front of the mirror and repeat your mantra aloud with enthusiasm while you brush your teeth. Yes, even with a mouth full of toothpaste! Let your reflection see your determination and feel your energy from the very start of the day.
- **Point:** Empower your morning routine with positive declarations.
  - **Example:** 'I am strong, I am confident, and I am ready to tackle the day.'
  - **Action:** Incorporate your affirmations into your shower routine. As the water cleanses you, let your words of affirmation wash over your mind, setting a powerful tone for the day ahead.

- **Point:** Transform your wake-up ritual with affirming thoughts.
  - **Example:** 'Every day, in every way, I am getting better and better.'
  - **Action:** Write your morning mantra on a sticky note and place it on your alarm clock. As you turn off your alarm, read the note aloud and let it fuel your morning motivation.

2. Gratitude Grabs:

- **Point:** Cultivate appreciation for life's little blessings.
  - **Example:** 'I'm grateful for my comfy bed, my morning coffee, and that random stranger who held the door for me.'
  - **Action:** Maintain a gratitude journal and jot down at least three things you're thankful for each day. Reflect on these entries before bed to end your day on a positive note.
- **Point:** Embrace thankfulness for everyday moments.
  - **Example:** 'I appreciate the warmth of the sun, the sound of birds singing, and the smile from a friend.'
  - **Action:** Create a gratitude jar and drop a note in it every time you feel thankful for something. Watch the jar fill up with positivity over time.
- **Point:** Recognize the beauty in the small joys of life.
  - **Example:** 'I'm thankful for the delicious breakfast I had, the helpful colleague, and the peaceful walk in the park.'
  - **Action:** Set a daily reminder on your phone to pause and think about what you are grateful for at that moment. Use these reminders to shift your focus to positivity throughout the day.

3. Visualization Vacation:

- **Point:** Picture your future success vividly.

- **Example:** Imagine yourself acing that presentation, running a marathon, or even nailing that tricky recipe.
- **Action:** Spend a few minutes daily visualizing your goals as already achieved. Make it vivid by incorporating all your senses – see the colors, hear the sounds, feel the emotions of success.

▶ **Point:** Envision your dreams turning into reality.
- **Example:** Picture yourself receiving that promotion, completing a challenging project, or enjoying a dream vacation.
- **Action:** Create a vision board with images and words representing your goals. Place it somewhere you'll see every day and take a moment to absorb its energy and inspiration.

▶ **Point:** Imagine your ambitions coming to fruition.
- **Example:** See yourself mastering a new skill, thriving in a new relationship, or living in your dream home.
- **Action:** Close your eyes and take a 'mental vacation' each day, where you fully immerse yourself in the experience of your future success. Feel the excitement and joy as if it's happening now.

4. Mental Reps:

▶ **Point:** Engage in daily mental exercises to keep your brain sharp.
- **Example:** Solve brainteasers, play strategy games, or learn something new each day.
- **Action:** Set aside a specific time each day for these activities, making it a fun and rewarding habit. Consider this your mental workout session.

▶ **Point:** Challenge your mind with stimulating activities.
- **Example:** Try crossword puzzles, chess, or Sudoku to keep your brain active.

- **Action:** Schedule a 'brain break' during your day where you focus solely on these activities. Treat it like a gym session for your mind.
- **Point:** Keep your cognitive skills in top shape with engaging tasks.
  - **Example:** Read challenging books, take up a new language, or tackle complex hobbies.
  - **Action:** Dedicate a portion of your daily routine to mental exercises. Rotate activities to keep things interesting and ensure a well-rounded mental workout.

5. Affirmation Apps and Tools:

- **Point:** Leverage technology to reinforce positivity.
  - **Example:** Apps like ThinkUp or Calm can send you daily affirmations and reminders.
  - **Action:** Download and use these apps to keep your affirmations fresh and engaging. Set up notifications to receive positive messages throughout the day.
- **Point:** Utilize digital tools to boost your affirmations.
  - **Example:** Apps such as Headspace and Reflectly can help you stay on track with your mental exercises.
  - **Action:** Integrate these apps into your daily routine, letting them guide your affirmation practice and provide timely reminders.
- **Point:** Enhance your mental routine with tech-savvy solutions.
  - **Example:** Use meditation and mindfulness apps to support your mental health journey.
  - **Action:** Regularly update your app settings to keep the content relevant and inspiring. Allow these tools to assist you in maintaining a consistent affirmation practice.

6. Mindful Moments:

- **Point:** Incorporate mindfulness into your day.

- **Example:** Take a deep breath and focus on the present moment, letting go of any stress or distractions.
- **Action:** Set aside a few minutes each day for mindfulness meditation. Focus on your breath, sensations, and surroundings to ground yourself in the present.

▶ **Point:** Practice mindfulness in daily activities.
- **Example:** Pay full attention while eating, savoring each bite, and noticing the flavors and textures.
- **Action:** Integrate mindfulness into routine tasks like walking, cooking, or even washing dishes. Be fully present in each activity.

▶ **Point:** Develop a mindful morning routine.
- **Example:** Start your day with a few moments of quiet reflection, setting a positive tone for the hours ahead.
- **Action:** Create a peaceful morning ritual that includes mindful breathing, stretching, and setting intentions for the day.

7. Positive Self-Talk:

▶ **Point:** Transform your inner dialogue.
- **Example:** Replace self-criticism with affirmations like 'I am capable and resilient.'
- **Action:** Monitor your thoughts and challenge any negative self-talk. Counter it with positive statements about your abilities and worth.

▶ **Point:** Reinforce a positive self-image.
- **Example:** Tell yourself, 'I am deserving of love and success.'
- **Action:** Stand in front of the mirror and speak kindly to yourself. Affirm your strengths and celebrate your achievements.

- **Point:** Cultivate a nurturing inner voice.
  - **Example:** Encourage yourself with phrases like 'I am doing my best and that's enough.'
  - **Action:** Practice self-compassion and gentleness in your thoughts. Treat yourself as you would a dear friend.

8. Empowering Habits:

- **Point:** Establish routines that boost your mental health.
  - **Example:** Start a daily meditation practice to calm your mind.
  - **Action:** Integrate empowering habits like reading, journaling, or exercising into your daily schedule. Make them non-negotiable parts of your routine.
- **Point:** Develop habits that foster growth.
  - **Example:** Spend time each day learning something new or enhancing a skill.
  - **Action:** Commit to continuous personal development. Set aside time for activities that challenge and inspire you.
- **Point:** Create a supportive environment for your habits.
  - **Example:** Design a peaceful space for your meditation or reading.
  - **Action:** Arrange your surroundings to encourage positive habits. Remove distractions and add elements that promote focus and relaxation.

9. Reflection and Growth:

- **Point:** Reflect on your progress regularly.
  - **Example:** Take time at the end of each week to review your achievements and areas for improvement.
  - **Action:** Keep a reflection journal where you document your thoughts, lessons learned, and goals for the future. Use it to track your growth over time.
- **Point:** Embrace the journey of self-improvement.

- **Example:** Celebrate small victories and learn from setbacks.
- **Action:** Set realistic goals and break them down into manageable steps. Acknowledge your progress and stay motivated.

▶ **Point:** Cultivate a growth mindset.
- **Example:** Believe that you can develop your abilities through effort and perseverance.
- **Action:** Approach challenges as opportunities for learning. Embrace feedback and use it to enhance your skills and understanding.

10. Self-Care Rituals:

▶ **Point:** Prioritize your well-being with regular self-care.
- **Example:** Take a relaxing bath, read a favorite book, or enjoy a hobby.
- **Action:** Schedule regular self-care activities that nurture your mind, body, and spirit. Treat them as essential parts of your routine.

▶ **Point:** Develop a holistic approach to self-care.
- **Example:** Incorporate physical, emotional, and mental self-care practices.
- **Action:** Balance activities like exercise, meditation, and socializing to address all aspects of your well-being.

▶ **Point:** Personalize your self-care routine.
- **Example:** Tailor your self-care practices to your unique needs and preferences.
- **Action:** Experiment with different activities and find what works best for you. Make adjustments as needed to ensure your self-care routine remains effective and enjoyable.

11. Inspirational Consumption:

- **Point:** Feed your mind with positive and uplifting content.
  - **Example:** Read motivational books, watch inspiring videos, or listen to uplifting podcasts.
  - **Action:** Curate a collection of content that inspires and motivates you. Dedicate time each day to consume and reflect on this material.
- **Point:** Seek out sources of inspiration.
  - **Example:** Follow thought leaders, authors, and influencers who share positive messages.
  - **Action:** Engage with content that aligns with your values and goals. Let it fuel your motivation and drive for self-improvement.
- **Point:** Balance consumption with creation.
  - **Example:** Apply the lessons and insights you gain from inspirational content to your own life.
  - **Action:** Use what you learn to set goals, make plans, and take action. Transform inspiration into tangible progress.

12. Connection and Community:

- **Point:** Build a supportive network.
  - **Example:** Surround yourself with positive, like-minded individuals who uplift and encourage you.
  - **Action:** Join groups, clubs, or online communities that share your interests and goals. Engage actively and build meaningful connections.
- **Point:** Foster meaningful relationships.
  - **Example:** Strengthen bonds with family and friends through quality time and open communication.
  - **Action:** Make an effort to connect regularly with your loved ones. Share your experiences, support each other, and grow together.
- **Point:** Contribute to your community.

- **Example:** Volunteer your time, skills, or resources to causes you care about.
- **Action:** Participate in community activities and initiatives. Give back and make a positive impact on those around you.

13. Goal Setting and Achievement:
- **Point:** Set clear, achievable goals.
  - **Example:** Define what success looks like for you and outline the steps to get there.
  - **Action:** Use SMART criteria (Specific, Measurable, Achievable, Relevant, Time-bound) to set your goals. Review and adjust them regularly.
- **Point:** Break goals into manageable tasks.
  - **Example:** Divide large goals into smaller, actionable steps.
  - **Action:** Create a detailed plan with timelines and milestones. Track your progress and celebrate each achievement.
- **Point:** Stay committed and focused.
  - **Example:** Maintain your motivation by reminding yourself of your goals and why they matter.
  - **Action:** Develop a daily routine that aligns with your objectives. Keep your goals visible and revisit them often to stay on track.

14. Creative Expression:
- **Point:** Tap into your creativity as a form of self-expression.
  - **Example:** Engage in activities like painting, writing, music, or dance.
  - **Action:** Schedule regular creative sessions where you can explore and express your artistic side. Let your creativity flow without judgement.

- **Point:** Use creativity to process emotions.
  - **Example:** Channel your feelings into your art, whether it's joy, sadness, or anything in between.
  - **Action:** Create a safe space for creative expression. Allow yourself to be vulnerable and authentic in your creative pursuits.
- **Point:** Integrate creativity into daily life.
  - **Example:** Find small ways to infuse creativity into your routine, like doodling, journaling, or cooking new recipes.
  - **Action:** Make creativity a habit by incorporating it into everyday activities. Embrace the joy and fulfillment it brings.

15. Nature Connection:

- **Point:** Reconnect with the natural world.
  - **Example:** Spend time outdoors, whether it's hiking, gardening, or simply sitting in a park.
  - **Action:** Schedule regular nature outings to refresh and recharge. Observe the beauty and tranquility of the natural environment.
- **Point:** Incorporate nature into your living space.
  - **Example:** Add plants, natural light, and outdoor elements to your home.
  - **Action:** Create a peaceful, nature-inspired environment that promotes relaxation and well-being.
- **Point:** Practice mindfulness in nature.
  - **Example:** Meditate or practice deep breathing while surrounded by nature.
  - **Action:** Use nature as a backdrop for mindfulness exercises. Let the sights, sounds, and smells of the natural world enhance your practice.

So, my dear positivity pirates, set sail on the seas of self-improvement! Overcome those limiting beliefs, mold your marvelous brain, and pump up your day with affirmations and exercises. Your mindset mastery awaits – onward to epicness!

3

The Time Sculptor–Mastering Time Management

Time management isn't just about cramming more tasks into your day; it's about creating a life where you feel fulfilled and accomplished.

Welcome, future Time Sculptor, to the enchanting world of mastering time management! Imagine you're an artist, and time is your medium. With the right tools and techniques, you can shape each day into a masterpiece. So, grab your chisel, don your artist's smock, and let's get sculpting!

Think of yourself as Michelangelo, but instead of carving marble, you're chiseling away at your daily schedule to reveal a perfectly balanced and productive masterpiece. Here's how we're going to make that happen.

Our goal is to transform how you perceive and utilize time. By the end of this journey, you'll be able to prioritize effectively, say no with confidence, and maximize productivity with ease.

Consider this the opening scene of an epic movie. You're the hero, and your mission, should you choose to accept it, is to master time management. Picture this: You're in a bustling marketplace. Vendors shout their wares, colors blur as people rush by, and yet, in the midst of chaos, you find a quiet corner to plan your strategy. That's what effective time management feels like – finding calm in the storm.

OVERCOMING THE OVERWHELM

Remember the time you felt completely overwhelmed with tasks, like you were juggling flaming swords while riding a unicycle on a tightrope over a pit of alligators? We've all been there. The sheer chaos can make even the simplest tasks feel impossible. Perhaps you were working on a big project, and every email felt like another flaming sword thrown your way. The phone rings, your boss asks for an urgent report, and just when you think it can't get any worse, your cat decides your keyboard is the perfect place for a nap.

Let's dive into a story that hits close to home. Meet Jane, an overworked manager at a bustling tech company. Jane was the epitome of 'busy but not productive.' Her desk was a battleground of sticky notes, her email inbox a minefield of unread messages, and her calendar looked like a Jackson Pollock painting with meetings splattered everywhere. Jane often stayed late at the office, only to realize she hadn't made a dent in her to-do list. Sound familiar?

One fateful Monday, after a weekend of zero relaxation and constant worrying about work, Jane decided enough was enough. She needed a change, and fast. That's when she stumbled upon the concept of prioritizing. It was like a beacon of light in her chaotic storm. She learned about the Eisenhower Matrix and decided to give it a try. Armed with nothing but determination and a strong cup of coffee, Jane categorized her tasks into urgent, important, and the rest.

The transformation was nothing short of miraculous. Jane

started her days by tackling the most important tasks first, those that would truly move the needle. She learned to say no to meetings that weren't essential and delegated tasks that didn't require her personal touch. Slowly but surely, Jane's chaotic days turned into structured, productive ones. Her email inbox became manageable, her desk clutter-free, and her work-life balance improved dramatically.

Jane's journey didn't stop there. She embraced other time management techniques, like time blocking and the Pomodoro Technique, and found that not only was she more productive, but she also had more free time to spend with her family and pursue hobbies. The once overwhelmed manager was now a beacon of productivity, inspiring her team to follow suit.

Just like Jane, you have the power to turn things around. The tools and techniques that transformed her life are at your disposal. Whether you're juggling multiple projects, dealing with constant interruptions, or simply trying to find a way to balance work and life, remember Jane's story. She was in the same boat, paddling furiously just to stay afloat. But with a bit of prioritization and some effective time management strategies, she became the captain of her own ship, navigating the seas of productivity with ease.

So, take a deep breath, grab your metaphorical chisel, and start shaping your time. You're not alone in this journey. Many have walked this path and emerged victorious. With the right mindset and tools, you too can transform your chaotic days into masterpieces of productivity. Welcome to the world of time sculpting!

Tips: This isn't just theoretical mumbo-jumbo. We're talking actionable advice you can start using today. For example, did you know that just five minutes of planning your day can save you hours of wasted effort? It's like sharpening your chisel before starting on that block of marble.

PRIORITIZING WHAT TRULY MATTERS

Mastering time management starts with identifying what's truly important in your life. It's easy to get lost in a sea of tasks and distractions, but with a clear focus, you can navigate your way to productivity nirvana.

1. **The Eisenhower Matrix:** Named after the 34th President of the United States, Dwight D. Eisenhower, this matrix helps you decide on and prioritize tasks by urgency and importance, sorting out less urgent and important tasks which you should either delegate or not spend much time on.
   - **Urgent and Important:** Tasks that need to be done immediately.
   - **Important, but Not Urgent:** Tasks that you can schedule to do later.
   - **Urgent, but Not Important:** Tasks that you can delegate to someone else.
   - **Not Urgent, Not Important:** Tasks that you can eliminate.
   - **Example:** Imagine your tasks as different-colored marbles. Urgent and important ones are red (handle immediately), important but not urgent are blue (schedule for later), urgent but not important are green (delegate or manage quickly), and neither urgent nor important are yellow (consider dropping). This visual helps you see where your focus should lie.
   - **Exercise:** Create your own Eisenhower Matrix. Write

down all your tasks and place them in the appropriate quadrant. You'll quickly see where your priorities should be.
2. **The Pareto Principle (80/20 Rule):** Named after economist Vilfredo Pareto, this principle suggests that 80% of your results come from 20% of your efforts. Focus on the tasks that bring the most value and results.
    - **Example:** If you're a writer, 20% of your efforts (like brainstorming and outlining) may yield 80% of the results (a well-structured article).
3. **ABCDE Method:** A classic method by time management expert Brian Tracy. Assign a letter to each task on your to-do list:
    - **A:** Must do – serious consequences if not done.
    - **B:** Should do – minor consequences if not done.
    - **C:** Nice to do – no consequences if not done.
    - **D:** Delegate – tasks that can be given to someone else.
    - **E:** Eliminate – tasks that are not necessary.
4. **The One Thing:** Inspired by Gary Keller's book, 'The One Thing,' this technique emphasizes focusing on the single most important task that will make everything else easier or unnecessary.
    - **Exercise:** Each morning, ask yourself, 'What's the one thing I can do today such that by doing it, everything else will be easier or unnecessary?'

THE ART OF SAYING NO

Learning to say no is a critical skill in time management. It's like being the gatekeeper of your own castle – you decide what enters your domain.

1. **The Polite Decline:** Sometimes, you can't take on additional tasks without compromising your priorities.
    - **Example:** 'I appreciate you thinking of me for this project, but I'm currently focusing on other priorities.'
    - **Example:** Think of a time when you overcommitted. Maybe you agreed to help a friend move, bake cookies for a school event, and finish a work project, all in one weekend. By Sunday night, you're exhausted, and none of the tasks got your best effort. Saying no to the less critical tasks would have allowed you to focus and excel.
    - **Exercise:** Practice saying no. Stand in front of a mirror and say, 'Thank you for thinking of me, but I have to decline.' Make it fun by imagining different scenarios: a demanding boss, a persuasive friend, or even a cute puppy with a calendar. Remember, it's not about rejecting people; it's about protecting your priorities.
2. **The Buffer Zone:** Creating a buffer zone between your commitments allows you to manage your time effectively.
    - **Exercise:** Before agreeing to new commitments, take a moment to assess your current workload and availability.
3. **The Sandwich Technique:** This technique involves cushioning your 'no' between two positives.
    - **Example:** 'I'm honored that you asked me to participate. Unfortunately, I won't be able to take on this project right now. However, I'm excited about the work you're doing and look forward to future opportunities.'
4. **The Redirection:** If you can't help, offer an alternative.
    - **Example:** 'I'm unable to help with this right now, but have you considered asking [Name]? They might have the capacity to assist.'

TECHNIQUES FOR MAXIMIZING PRODUCTIVITY

Becoming a master Time Sculptor means using proven techniques to maximize your productivity. Here are some tools and strategies to keep your chisel sharp:

1. **Time Blocking:** This involves scheduling specific blocks of time for different tasks or activities.
   - **Example:** Dedicate 9-11 AM to focused work, 11-12 PM for meetings, and 1-2 PM for emails and admin tasks.
   - **Example:** Picture yourself in a kitchen. Each task is a different dish, and you're the master chef orchestrating a flawless meal. Time Blocking is your menu, ensuring you know when to start each dish. The Pomodoro Technique is your timer, making sure nothing burns while keeping you on track.
   - **Exercise:** Start with a weekly Time Block. List your main tasks and assign them time slots. Use the Pomodoro Technique for focused tasks, setting a timer for 25 minutes and taking a 5-minute break when it rings. Gradually adjust as you find what works best for you.
2. **Pomodoro Technique:** Developed by Francesco Cirillo, this technique uses a timer to break work into intervals, traditionally 25 minutes in length, separated by short breaks.
   - **Exercise:** Work for 25 minutes, then take a 5-minute break. Repeat this cycle four times, then take a longer break (15-30 minutes).
3. **The 2-Minute Rule:** From David Allen's 'Getting Things Done,' if a task takes two minutes or less, do it immediately.
   - **Example:** Respond to a quick email or file a document.
4. **The Ivy Lee Method:** At the end of each workday, write down the six most important things you need to accomplish

tomorrow, prioritizing them by importance. Focus on completing each task one at a time in the order listed.
   - **Exercise:** Spend the last 10 minutes of your day planning for the next.
5. **Eat That Frog:** Inspired by Mark Twain's saying, 'Eat a live frog first thing in the morning and nothing worse will happen to you the rest of the day.' Tackle your most challenging task first.
   - **Exercise:** Identify your 'frog' each morning and tackle it before anything else.
6. **Batching:** Group similar tasks together to streamline your workflow and reduce the mental energy needed to switch between different types of tasks.
   - **Example:** Batch all your emails, calls, or errands together.
7. **Automation and Delegation**: Use tools and delegate tasks to free up your time for more critical work.
   - **Example:** Use automation tools for repetitive tasks and delegate non-essential tasks to others.
8. **Review and Reflect:** Regularly reviewing your progress and reflecting on what works and what doesn't helps improve your time management skills.
   - **Exercise:** Spend time at the end of each week reviewing your accomplishments and planning for the next week.
9. **Digital Detox:** Limit distractions by managing your digital consumption.
   - **Exercise:** Schedule specific times for checking emails and social media, and use apps that block distracting sites during work hours.
10. **Environmental Design:** Create a workspace that minimizes distractions and enhances focus.
    - **Example:** Keep your workspace tidy, use noise-canceling headphones, and ensure good lighting.

ADDING HUMOUR TO YOUR TIME SCULPTING JOURNEY

1. **The Battle of the Procrastinators:**
   - Imagine your brain is a kingdom, and you're the ruler. One day, you declare war on the Procrastination Army. You, the valiant Time Sculptor, wield your trusty sword of Planning. 'To arms!' you cry, and your loyal neurons march into battle, armed with planners and to-do lists. It's a tough fight, but with strategic breaks and focused work sessions, you vanquish the Procrastination Army, reclaiming your kingdom one task at a time.
2. **The Tale of the Perpetual Planner:**
   - Picture a character who spends so much time planning their day that they forget to actually do anything. They've got color-coded schedules, intricate mind maps, and enough sticky notes to wallpaper a room. One day, they discover the power of simplicity – a straightforward to-do list. Suddenly, they're not just planning; they're doing. And oh, the joy of crossing off tasks!
3. **The Office Olympics:**
   - Ever heard of the Office Olympics? It's where time management skills are put to the test in hilarious ways. Events include the Email Relay (respond as fast as you can), the Meeting Marathon (stay focused in the longest meeting ever), and the Deadline Dash (complete tasks just before the clock runs out). The gold medal? A day where you leave the office on time, with everything done.

QUESTIONS FOR REFLECTION:

- What tasks currently fill your day? Are they urgent, important, or neither?
- When was the last time you said no to protect your time?
- How do you currently organize your tasks? Could you benefit from techniques like Time Blocking or the Pomodoro Technique?

INTERACTIVE ELEMENTS:

- **Quiz:** What's Your Time Management Style? (Are you a Planner, a Doer, or a Dreamer?)
- **Checklist:** Daily Time Sculpting Checklist to help you stay on track.
- **Challenge:** The 7-Day Time Management Challenge – Implement one new strategy each day and reflect on your progress.

'Today, choose one technique to implement and see how it transforms your productivity. Start small, but think big!'

FINAL VERDICT: YOUR MAGNUM OPUS AWAITS

Well, well, well, look at you, Time Sculptor Extraordinaire! You've delved into the labyrinth of time management and emerged victorious, armed with an arsenal of strategies to conquer your day. Picture yourself as a maestro with a palette of vibrant colors, ready to paint your masterpiece on the canvas of life. The possibilities are endless, and the brush is in your hand.

Let's get real—time is your most precious resource. Unlike money, you can't stash away minutes for a rainy day. Once a moment's gone, it's gone for good. So, mastering time management isn't just a skill; it's a superpower. By prioritizing what's important, mastering the art of saying 'no,' and using productivity hacks, you can turn your life from a chaotic mess into a symphony of success.

Prioritize Like a Pro Imagine your day as a wild jungle. There's a ton of foliage, but only a few plants bear the juiciest fruits. Prioritizing is like deciding which plants to water and which to let wilt. With tools like the Eisenhower Matrix and the Pareto Principle, you can spot the tasks that really matter and focus on those. No more getting lost in the weeds—you're all about harvesting those big, sweet successes.

Master the Magic Word: 'No' Learning to say 'no' is like guarding the gates of your own personal fortress. It's not about rejecting people or opportunities; it's about protecting your time and energy. Every time you say 'yes' to something that doesn't align with your goals, you're essentially saying 'no' to something that does. So, get comfy with the word 'no'—it's your shield against the invasion of unnecessary tasks.

Optimize Like a Boss Think of your day as a high-performance race car. Regular tune-ups, slick tyres, and top-notch fuel keep it running smoothly. Techniques like Time Blocking, the Pomodoro Technique, and the 2-Minute Rule are your pit crew. Time Blocking helps you dedicate specific slots for tasks, Pomodoro keeps you focused with work sprints and breaks, and the 2-Minute Rule zaps small tasks before they pile up into a mountain.

Embrace Your Inner Sculptor You're not just managing time; you're sculpting it. Each day starts as a block of marble, rough and full of potential. With your newfound skills, you can chisel away the unnecessary and shape your day into a masterpiece of productivity and joy. Every decision, every task you prioritize, and every distraction you dodge brings you closer to your ideal day.

Onward with Precision and Panache So, stride forward with confidence and flair. Tackle each day with the knowledge that you have the tools to triumph. Celebrate your wins, learn from your setbacks, and keep honing your craft. Remember, mastering time management is a journey, not a destination. There will always be new tricks to learn and distractions to conquer, but you've got the foundation to handle whatever comes your way.

Look to the wisdom of time management legends who came before you. Let their stories and strategies inspire you to keep pushing forward. Your dedication will pay off, and you'll reap the rewards in a balanced, efficient, and deeply satisfying life.

Congratulations again, Time Sculptor. Your magnificent creation awaits. Now, grab your chisel and start sculpting the life you've always dreamed of. Happy sculpting!

DAILY PRACTICES AND
EMOTIONAL WELL-BEING

Picture this: You're a superhero. No, not the cape-wearing kind. You're the type of superhero who defeats procrastination, vanquishes laziness, and battles the evil forces of 'I'll do it later.' Your superpower? Daily habits. Yes, those seemingly small, mundane actions that, when done consistently, turn you into an unstoppable force of nature. Imagine waking up each day with a clear sense of purpose, a roadmap for your journey, and a toolkit brimming with habits that make each step forward feel almost effortless. These daily habits are your secret weapons, finely tuned to combat the distractions and obstacles that threaten to derail your mission. They are the unsung heroes of your routine, the steady undercurrent of discipline and structure that propels you toward your goals with unwavering determination.

Daily habits are like the secret recipe in grandma's famous chocolate chip cookies—simple yet profound. They're the reason why successful people seem to glide through life effortlessly while the rest of us scramble to find our keys every morning. Developing good habits can transform your life from chaotic to organized, from stressful to serene, and from mediocre to magnificent. Consider the magic that happens when you automate the good decisions that lead to success. Each day, your habits shape your actions, and your actions shape your destiny. This process is not instantaneous but gradual, akin to the way a river carves a canyon over millennia. Every small action, repeated consistently, has a cumulative effect, creating a powerful momentum that drives you forward.

4

The Habit Builder–Constructing a Routine for Success

The journey to greatness begins with these small, often overlooked choices. Brushing your teeth, making your bed, or starting your day with a few moments of mindfulness might seem trivial, but these actions set the tone for the rest of your day. They establish a pattern of discipline and attention to detail that permeates every aspect of your life. By mastering these small tasks, you build a foundation of reliability and consistency. Think of daily habits as the building blocks of your character. Each habit you cultivate is a testament to your commitment to excellence. Over time, these habits become second nature, ingrained so deeply in your routine that you perform them without conscious effort. This automation frees up mental energy, allowing you to focus on more complex and creative endeavors. Your mind becomes a well-oiled machine, primed for innovation and problem-solving.

Moreover, daily habits serve as a buffer against the chaos of life. When unexpected challenges arise, your habits provide a sense of stability and control. They anchor you, offering a familiar rhythm that can be relied upon even in turbulent times. This stability is crucial for maintaining a positive mindset and ensuring that setbacks do not derail your progress. The beauty of daily habits lies in their simplicity. They do not require extraordinary talent or resources, just a willingness to commit and the perseverance to follow through. Each habit, no matter how small, contributes to a larger picture of success. Like drops of water filling a bucket, they accumulate, gradually transforming your life.

Consider the impact of a habit like reading for 30 minutes each day. Initially, it might seem insignificant—a mere blip in your daily schedule. However, over a year, this habit amounts to over 180 hours of reading. That's 180 hours of learning, growth, and intellectual stimulation. The knowledge and insights gained during this time can have a profound impact on your personal and professional development. Or take the habit of exercising regularly. A short workout each day might feel inconsequential, but the cumulative effect on your health and well-being is substantial. Regular exercise boosts your energy levels, enhances your mood, and improves your overall fitness. It's an investment in your physical and mental health that pays dividends over a lifetime.

BUILDING A MORNING ROUTINE THAT ENERGIZES

Ever wonder why some people are morning people, and others look like they've been attacked by a grizzly bear before their first cup of coffee? It's all about the morning routine, my friend. Let's craft one that doesn't just get you out of bed but launches you into the day like a rocket.

1. **Wake Up with Purpose**: Start by setting your alarm for a consistent time that ensures you get enough sleep. This is not just about avoiding the snooze button—it's about

establishing a rhythm that aligns with your body's natural circadian rhythms. When you wake up at the same time each day, your body adjusts, making it easier to rise and shine. The goal here is to wake up with a sense of purpose, ready to seize the day.

As soon as your alarm goes off, resist the temptation to hit snooze. Think of each snooze as a delay in the start of your mission. You're not just hitting pause on your life; you're postponing your potential. Instead, get up immediately, stretching your body to signal that it's time to start the day. This initial act of discipline sets a positive tone, reinforcing your commitment to a productive day.

2. **Stretch and Move**: Before you even think about checking your phone and diving into the digital abyss, take a moment to stretch your body. Gentle stretching helps to wake up your muscles and improve circulation. Consider incorporating a short yoga session or a quick workout into your routine. These activities not only help to wake up your body but also release endorphins, which enhance your mood and energy levels.

   Imagine your body as a machine that needs to be warmed up before it can function at its best. Stretching and moving first thing in the morning is like hitting the refresh button, preparing your body for the day ahead. This practice can also help alleviate any stiffness from the night's sleep, ensuring you start your day feeling physically ready to take on whatever comes your way.

3. **Hydrate and Fuel**: After several hours of sleep, your body is naturally dehydrated. Start your day by drinking a glass of water to kickstart your metabolism and rehydrate your system. Water is essential for all bodily functions, and starting your day with hydration helps to wake up your

organs and improve your alertness.

Follow this up with a nutritious breakfast. Think of breakfast as fueling your superpower engine. Opt for foods that provide sustained energy, such as whole grains, fruits, and proteins. Avoid sugary cereals and pastries, which can cause energy crashes later in the day. Instead, choose a balanced meal that keeps you full and energized throughout the morning. Consider foods like oatmeal with fresh fruit, a smoothie packed with greens and protein, or eggs with whole-grain toast and avocado.

4. **Mindfulness and Planning**: Spend a few minutes meditating or practicing mindfulness. This helps to clear the cobwebs from your brain and sets a calm, focused tone for the day. Mindfulness practices can include deep breathing exercises, guided meditation, or simply sitting quietly and observing your thoughts.

    Once you've centered yourself, take some time to plan your day. Write down your top priorities and outline the tasks you need to accomplish. This is your battle plan. By having a clear idea of what you need to do, you reduce the risk of feeling overwhelmed and increase your chances of staying on track. Use tools like planners, to-do lists, or digital apps to organize your tasks. Prioritize them based on urgency and importance, ensuring that you tackle the most critical tasks first.

5. **Personal Growth**: Dedicate a portion of your morning to personal growth. This could be reading a chapter from a book, listening to an inspiring podcast, or watching a motivational video. Feed your brain before you feed the chaos. Personal growth activities not only expand your knowledge but also provide motivation and inspiration for the day ahead.

Think of this time as an investment in yourself. By continuously learning and growing, you equip yourself with the tools and mindset needed to navigate the challenges of the day. Choose materials that align with your goals and interests, whether they're related to your career, personal development, or hobbies. This practice ensures that you start your day with a positive and proactive mindset.

6. **Connect with Loved Ones**: If possible, use a part of your morning to connect with loved ones. A brief conversation with a family member, a hug from your partner, or a moment spent with your pet can boost your mood and provide emotional support. These small interactions help to strengthen your relationships and remind you of the important people in your life.

7. **Creative Expression**: Allow some time for creative expression. Whether it's writing in a journal, doodling, playing a musical instrument, or engaging in any other form of creativity, this practice can be incredibly energizing. Creativity stimulates your brain, improves your problem-solving skills, and can provide a sense of fulfillment and joy. It's a way to express yourself and tap into your inner resources before the busyness of the day begins.

8. **Review and Adjust**: As you go through your morning routine, periodically review and adjust it. What works for you might change over time, and that's okay. Stay flexible and open to tweaking your routine to better suit your evolving needs and circumstances. The key is consistency, but within that framework, there's room for adaptation and improvement.

9. **Reflect on Your Why**: Take a moment each morning to reflect on your goals and aspirations. Remind yourself why you're committed to your routine and what you're working toward. This reflection can provide a deeper sense

of motivation and drive, helping you to stay focused on your long-term vision.
10. **Gratitude Practice**: Incorporate a gratitude practice into your morning. Reflect on things you're thankful for and write them down. This simple act can shift your perspective, fostering a positive mindset and reducing stress. Gratitude can improve your emotional well-being and set a positive tone for the rest of the day.

THE COMPREHENSIVE MORNING ROUTINE

Combining all these elements, a comprehensive morning routine might look something like this:

1. **Wake Up with Purpose**: Set your alarm and rise without hitting snooze.
2. **Stretch and Move**: Engage in a 15-minute yoga session or a quick workout.
3. **Hydrate and Fuel**: Drink a glass of water and enjoy a nutritious breakfast.
4. **Mindfulness and Planning**: Spend 10 minutes meditating and then plan your day.
5. **Personal Growth**: Read a book or listen to a podcast for 15-20 minutes.
6. **Connect with Loved Ones**: Share a few moments with family or pets.
7. **Creative Expression**: Engage in a creative activity for 10-15 minutes.
8. **Review and Adjust**: Periodically evaluate and tweak your routine.
9. **Reflect on Your Why**: Remind yourself of your goals and motivations.

10. Gratitude Practice: Write down three things you're grateful for.

By incorporating these practices into your morning routine, you create a powerful start to your day, setting yourself up for success and fulfillment. This routine ensures that you not only start your day with energy and focus but also with a sense of purpose and positivity. Each element of the routine is designed to nourish your mind, body, and soul, preparing you to tackle the challenges and seize the opportunities that lie ahead.

EVENING RITUALS FOR REFLECTION AND GROWTH

As the sun sets and you hang up your superhero cape for the day, it's time to reflect and prepare for tomorrow. Evening rituals are your cooldown, the epilogue to your daily adventure. They provide a structured way to wind down, reflect, and reset, ensuring that you close out each day with a sense of accomplishment and peace.

1. **Review the Day**: Begin by reflecting on the events of the day. Take a moment to think about what went well and what didn't. Celebrate your victories, no matter how small they may seem. This practice is crucial because it helps you recognize your progress and reinforces positive behavior. Additionally, acknowledging the challenges you face provides valuable learning opportunities. Instead of focusing on what went wrong, think about what you can learn from those experiences. This reflection time allows you to internalize the day's lessons and prepare to apply them in the future. To enhance this reflection, consider keeping a journal. Writing down your thoughts can help clarify them and make your reflections more concrete. You might write about

specific achievements, moments of joy, and lessons learned from mistakes. Over time, this journal can become a valuable resource, documenting your growth and progress.

2. **Gratitude Practice**: Gratitude is a powerful tool for improving your mood and overall well-being. Each evening, write down three things you're grateful for. This practice can be likened to taking a happy pill before bed, but without the weird side effects. It shifts your focus from what's lacking in your life to what you have, fostering a positive mindset. Your gratitude list doesn't have to include monumental things; it can be as simple as appreciating a beautiful sunset, a delicious meal, or a kind word from a friend. The key is to make this practice consistent. Over time, you'll find that it becomes easier to identify things you're grateful for, and this habit will cultivate a more positive outlook on life.

3. **Plan Tomorrow**: Before you go to bed, take a few minutes to look at your to-do list for the next day. Prioritize your tasks and set your intentions. You're not just going to sleep; you're recharging for another epic day. By planning ahead, you create a roadmap for the day, which can reduce stress and increase productivity.

   In addition to listing tasks, consider setting specific goals for the day. What do you want to achieve? What steps will you take to get there? Setting clear goals helps to focus your efforts and makes it more likely that you'll accomplish what you set out to do. This planning session can also help you identify any potential obstacles and think about how to overcome them.

4. **Wind Down**: Create a bedtime routine that signals to your body that it's time to sleep. Avoid screens at least an hour before bed, as the blue light emitted by phones, tablets, and computers can interfere with your sleep cycle. Instead,

The Habit Builder–Constructing a Routine for Success 63

engage in calming activities that help you relax.
Consider reading a book, taking a warm bath, or listening to calming music. These activities can help lower your stress levels and prepare your body for sleep. You might also try practicing some light stretching or yoga to release any tension built up during the day. The goal is to create a series of activities that you enjoy and that help you transition smoothly from wakefulness to sleepiness.

5. **Sleep Well**: Ensure you get 7-8 hours of quality sleep. Your brain and body need this time to repair and prepare for the next day's adventures. Good sleep hygiene is essential for maintaining overall health and well-being. In addition to having a consistent bedtime, make sure your sleep environment is conducive to rest. Keep your bedroom cool, dark, and quiet, and invest in a comfortable mattress and pillows.
   If you find it difficult to fall asleep, try incorporating relaxation techniques such as deep breathing, progressive muscle relaxation, or guided imagery. These practices can help calm your mind and body, making it easier to drift off to sleep. Remember, quality sleep is just as important as quantity, so focus on creating an environment and routine that promotes restful sleep.

6. **Disconnect to Reconnect**: In our hyper-connected world, it's easy to stay glued to screens right up until bedtime. However, disconnecting from digital devices is crucial for a restful evening. Instead of scrolling through social media or checking emails, use this time to reconnect with yourself and your loved ones. Engage in meaningful conversations, share stories, or simply enjoy each other's company.
   This period of disconnection can also be a time for self-care. Practice mindfulness or meditation to center yourself and

let go of the day's stress. Focus on your breathing, observe your thoughts without judgement, and allow yourself to be present in the moment. This practice not only enhances relaxation but also fosters a sense of inner peace.

7. **Set a Relaxing Environment**: Your bedroom environment plays a significant role in the quality of your sleep. Create a space that promotes relaxation and tranquility. Use blackout curtains to block out light, invest in a white noise machine to drown out any disruptive sounds, and consider using calming scents like lavender or chamomile.

    Additionally, declutter your bedroom to create a serene atmosphere. A tidy space can help clear your mind and make it easier to unwind. Make your bed each morning so that when you return in the evening, your bed feels inviting and ready for rest.

8. **Reflect and Release**: As you wind down, take a moment to reflect on the emotional highs and lows of the day. Acknowledge any negative emotions or stressful events, and then consciously release them. Holding onto negative emotions can affect your sleep quality and overall well-being. One effective way to release these emotions is through writing. Keep a journal by your bedside and write about anything that's on your mind. This practice can help you process your thoughts and let go of any lingering stress. By the time you go to bed, you'll have a clearer, more peaceful mind.

9. **Nourish Your Body and Soul**: Consider incorporating a nourishing activity into your evening routine. This could be anything that makes you feel good and rejuvenates your spirit. Perhaps it's a cup of herbal tea, a soothing face mask, or a few minutes of creative expression through drawing or writing.

    Nourishing activities can also include self-compassion

practices. Spend a few moments appreciating yourself and acknowledging your efforts. Recognize that it's okay to have off days and that you're doing your best. This practice fosters a positive relationship with yourself and promotes emotional well-being.

10. **Visualize Tomorrow's Success**: As you lie in bed, take a few minutes to visualize your success for the coming day. Imagine yourself confidently tackling tasks, overcoming challenges, and achieving your goals. Visualization can be a powerful tool for setting a positive mindset and preparing your brain for success.

Picture the steps you'll take, the obstacles you might face, and how you'll navigate them. By mentally rehearsing your day, you build confidence and reduce anxiety. This practice also helps reinforce your intentions and goals, making it more likely that you'll accomplish what you set out to do.

THE COMPREHENSIVE EVENING ROUTINE

Combining all these elements, a comprehensive evening routine might look something like this:

1. **Review the Day**: Reflect on your accomplishments and challenges.
2. **Gratitude Practice**: Write down three things you're grateful for.
3. **Plan Tomorrow**: Outline your tasks and set your goals for the next day.
4. **Wind Down**: Engage in calming activities like reading, bathing, or listening to music.
5. **Sleep Well**: Ensure your sleep environment is comfortable and conducive to rest.

6. **Disconnect to Reconnect**: Spend time away from screens and connect with loved ones.
7. **Set a Relaxing Environment**: Create a peaceful bedroom environment.
8. **Reflect and Release**: Journal your thoughts and release any lingering stress.
9. **Nourish Your Body and Soul**: Incorporate self-care and nourishing activities.
10. **Visualize Tomorrow's Success**: Mentally rehearse the next day's successes.

By incorporating these practices into your evening routine, you set the stage for a restful night and a productive, positive day ahead. Each element of the routine is designed to help you unwind, reflect, and recharge, ensuring that you close out each day with a sense of peace and preparation for the adventures that await.

THE SECRET SAUCE: CONSISTENCY AND FLEXIBILITY

Here's the kicker—consistency is key. But, life is unpredictable. Sometimes, the villain of chaos sneaks into your day, and routines get disrupted. Flexibility is your sidekick. Adapt and adjust without losing sight of your goals. Remember, even superheroes have off days. It's essential to understand that the journey to success is not a straight line but a series of twists and turns, peaks and valleys. The key to navigating this complex terrain lies in balancing steadfast consistency with adaptable flexibility.

Consistency is the backbone of habit formation. It's the relentless commitment to show up every day, to put in the effort, and to stay the course even when it's challenging. It's about creating a rhythm and routine that become second nature over time. Consistency breeds familiarity and reliability, which are crucial for building and maintaining habits. However, this does not mean being rigid or inflexible.

Flexibility, on the other hand, is the ability to bend without breaking. It's the capacity to adapt to changes, to pivot when necessary, and to embrace the unexpected without losing momentum. Life is dynamic, full of unforeseen events that can throw a wrench in your plans. A flexible approach allows you to navigate these disruptions smoothly. When consistency meets flexibility, you create a resilient framework that can withstand the ebb and flow of life's unpredictability.

Imagine your journey as a dance between consistency and flexibility. Consistency provides the steady beat, the underlying rhythm that keeps you moving forward. Flexibility adds the fluidity and grace, allowing you to navigate around obstacles and adapt to changes without losing your footing. Together, they form a harmonious balance that enables sustainable progress.

PRACTICAL TIPS AND TRICKS

To harness the power of both consistency and flexibility, here are some practical tips and tricks to guide you:

- **Start Small**: Don't try to overhaul your entire life in one go. Pick one habit and stick to it. Once it's solid, add another. Starting small reduces the risk of feeling overwhelmed and increases the likelihood of success. It's about building a strong foundation before adding more layers. For example, if you want to incorporate exercise into your routine, start with a 10-minute walk each day. Gradually increase the duration and intensity as the habit becomes ingrained.
- **Use Reminders**: Sticky notes, phone alarms, or apps—use

whatever it takes to remind you of your habits. Reminders help keep your goals at the forefront of your mind, ensuring that you don't forget or overlook them. Place sticky notes in visible locations, set alarms on your phone, or use habit-tracking apps to stay on top of your commitments. The key is to create cues that trigger the desired behavior.

- **Find Accountability**: Share your goals with a friend or join a community. Accountability partners are like your superhero squad. They provide support, encouragement, and a sense of responsibility. Knowing that someone else is aware of your goals and progress can be a powerful motivator. Consider joining a group with similar interests or finding a buddy who shares your aspirations. Regular check-ins and updates can help keep you on track.
- **Reward Yourself**: Celebrate your wins. Rewards can be small but meaningful. Maybe a treat, a break, or a little dance party. Recognizing and celebrating your achievements, no matter how small, reinforces positive behavior and keeps you motivated. Rewards provide a sense of accomplishment and enjoyment, making the process of habit formation more enjoyable. Choose rewards that are meaningful to you and that genuinely make you feel good.

THE ROLE OF MINDSET

Your mindset plays a crucial role in balancing consistency and flexibility. Adopting a growth mindset—a belief that your abilities and habits can be developed through dedication and hard work—can significantly impact your success. With a growth mindset, setbacks and challenges are seen as opportunities for learning and growth rather than as failures.

- **Embrace Imperfection**: Understand that perfection is not the goal. Striving for perfection can lead to frustration and burnout. Instead, aim for progress. Celebrate small victories and recognize that every step forward, no matter how small, is a step in the right direction. Embracing imperfection allows you to stay motivated and resilient in the face of challenges.
- **Be Kind to Yourself**: Treat yourself with the same compassion and understanding that you would offer a friend. When you encounter setbacks or make mistakes, avoid self-criticism. Instead, acknowledge your efforts and learn from the experience. Self-compassion fosters resilience and helps you bounce back more effectively.
- **Stay Flexible in Your Approach**: If a particular strategy isn't working, be willing to adjust your approach. Flexibility means being open to trying new methods and finding what works best for you. It's about adapting your strategies to fit your evolving needs and circumstances. For example, if your morning routine becomes too hectic, experiment with different time slots or activities until you find a rhythm that suits you.

PRACTICAL STRATEGIES FOR BUILDING CONSISTENCY

To build consistency, consider the following strategies:

- **Create a Routine**: Establish a daily or weekly routine that incorporates your desired habits. Consistency thrives on routine. By setting specific times and triggers for your habits, you make it easier to stick to them. For instance, if you want to develop a reading habit, schedule a specific time each day for reading, such as before bed or during

your lunch break.
- **Set Clear Goals**: Define your goals clearly and break them down into actionable steps. Having a clear vision of what you want to achieve provides direction and motivation. Break your goals into smaller, manageable tasks that you can tackle one at a time. This approach makes the overall goal less daunting and more achievable.
- **Track Your Progress**: Use a journal, app, or calendar to track your progress. Monitoring your habits helps you stay accountable and provides a visual representation of your achievements. Seeing your progress can boost your motivation and encourage you to keep going. Regularly reviewing your progress also allows you to identify patterns and make adjustments as needed.
- **Stay Consistent with Your Environment**: Design your environment to support your habits. Remove distractions and create spaces that facilitate your goals. For example, if you want to eat healthier, keep nutritious snacks readily available and remove unhealthy options from your immediate surroundings. An environment that supports your habits makes it easier to stay consistent.

EMBRACING FLEXIBILITY

While consistency is essential, flexibility ensures that you can adapt to changing circumstances without derailing your progress. Here's how to embrace flexibility effectively:

- **Have Backup Plans**: Life is unpredictable, and things don't always go as planned. Have backup plans in place for your habits. If you can't make it to the gym, have a home workout routine ready. If you miss your morning meditation, find a

quiet moment during the day to practice. Having alternatives ensures that you can maintain your habits even when faced with unexpected challenges.
- **Adjust Your Goals**: Be willing to adjust your goals based on your current situation. Sometimes, life demands more flexibility, and it's okay to modify your goals accordingly. For example, during busy periods, you might reduce the duration of your exercise routine but still commit to doing some form of physical activity. The key is to stay adaptable and maintain the essence of the habit.
- **Practice Mindfulness**: Mindfulness helps you stay present and aware of your thoughts and emotions. When disruptions occur, mindfulness allows you to respond thoughtfully rather than react impulsively. By practicing mindfulness, you can better navigate challenges and make conscious choices that align with your goals. Take a few moments each day to check in with yourself and assess how you're feeling. This practice can enhance your ability to adapt and stay on track.

Incorporating both consistency and flexibility into your habit-building process creates a powerful synergy. Consistency lays the foundation for lasting habits, while flexibility ensures that you can navigate life's unpredictability without losing sight of your goals. Together, they form a resilient and adaptable approach that empowers you to achieve sustainable success.

Embrace the power of habits, and you'll find yourself achieving more with less effort. Your morning routine will become the launchpad for your daily adventures, and your evening rituals will ensure you're ready for the next day's challenges. So, put on your superhero mask, and let your habits be the secret weapon that propels you towards success. Remember, every small action counts, and together, they create the masterpiece of your life.

And also remember, even superheroes have off days. What matters is your ability to adapt, learn, and continue moving forward. Embrace the journey with a balanced approach, and you'll find yourself not only achieving your goals but also growing and evolving along the way.

5

Emotional Engineer–Designing Emotional Resilience

WELCOME TO EMOTIONAL ENGINEERING

Imagine being an emotional engineer. Picture it: you're wearing a hard hat, a toolbox in hand, filled not with wrenches and screwdrivers but with tissues and inspirational quotes. Welcome to the workshop of your mind, where we'll be designing and building the most resilient emotional skyscraper ever seen.

THE BLUEPRINT OF EMOTIONAL RESILIENCE

Building emotional resilience starts with a solid blueprint. Just like an architect wouldn't start constructing a skyscraper without detailed plans, we need a clear design for our emotional framework.

1. **Foundation of Self-Awareness**
   - **Understanding Your Emotions**: Self-awareness is the bedrock of emotional resilience. Start by recognizing and labeling your emotions. Are you feeling anxious,

excited, or perhaps a mix of both? Understanding what you feel is the first step towards managing those feelings effectively.
- **Case Study: Emotional Audit**: Think of Sarah, a project manager who always seemed overwhelmed. After keeping an emotional journal for a month, she realized that her stress peaks every time she has to present at meetings. This insight helped her focus on improving her public speaking skills, significantly reducing her anxiety.

2. **Framework of Self-Regulation**
   - **Emotional Regulation Techniques**: Just as engineers use beams and supports to stabilize a structure, emotional regulation techniques stabilize our reactions. Techniques like deep breathing, mindfulness, and cognitive reappraisal help manage intense emotions.
   - **Example: Deep Breathing Exercise**: Imagine Tom, a software developer who used to panic during tight deadlines. By practicing deep breathing exercises, he learned to calm his mind, allowing him to think clearly and meet his deadlines efficiently.

3. **Walls of Social Awareness**
   - **Empathy and Understanding**: Building walls in a skyscraper is akin to developing social awareness in emotional engineering. Empathy allows us to understand and relate to others' emotions, creating strong, supportive relationships.
   - **Story: Walking in Their Shoes**: Consider Emily, a teacher who struggled to connect with her students. By taking time to understand their backgrounds and challenges, she built stronger relationships, improving the classroom environment for everyone.

4. **Roof of Relationship Management**

- **Building Strong Relationships**: The roof of your emotional skyscraper is constructed by managing relationships effectively. This involves clear communication, conflict resolution, and building trust.
- **Example: Conflict Resolution**: Meet Jack, a team leader who often found himself in the middle of team disputes. By learning and applying conflict resolution strategies, he transformed his team's dynamics, fostering a more collaborative and positive work environment.

TOOLS OF THE TRADE

Every engineer needs the right tools, and emotional engineers are no different. Let's explore some essential tools for your emotional toolbox:

1. **Mindfulness and Meditation**
   - **Daily Practice**: Mindfulness and meditation are like the precision instruments in your toolbox. They help you stay present and grounded, reducing stress and enhancing emotional clarity.
   - **Example: Morning Meditation Routine**: Lucy, a marketing executive, started her day with a 10-minute meditation. This practice helped her approach each day with a calm and focused mindset, improving her productivity and overall well-being.
2. **Positive Affirmations**
   - **Building Self-Esteem**: Positive affirmations act as the reinforcing steel in your emotional structure. They boost your self-esteem and resilience by encouraging positive self-talk.
   - **Example: Affirmation Journal**: John, a college student,

wrote down three positive affirmations every night before bed. Over time, he noticed a significant improvement in his confidence and reduced feelings of self-doubt.

3. **Gratitude Practice**
   - **Enhancing Positivity**: Gratitude is like the cement that holds your emotional building blocks together. Regularly acknowledging what you are grateful for increases overall happiness and emotional strength.
   - **Story: Gratitude Jar**: Mary, a busy mom, kept a gratitude jar. Every day, she wrote something she was grateful for and put it in the jar. This simple practice helped her maintain a positive outlook, even on the toughest days.

THEORIES AND INSIGHTS

1. **Maslow's Hierarchy of Needs**
   - **Application in Emotional Engineering**: Just as engineers consider the fundamental principles of physics, emotional engineers can apply psychological theories like Maslow's Hierarchy of Needs. Ensuring basic needs are met creates a stable foundation for higher-level emotional development.
   - **Example: Workplace Application**: In a corporate setting, ensuring employees' basic needs (fair wages, safe working conditions) are met can foster a sense of belonging and self-actualization, leading to higher productivity and job satisfaction.
2. **Cognitive Behavioral Theory (CBT)**
   - **Changing Thought Patterns**: CBT principles can be employed to reframe negative thoughts and behaviors, much like an engineer might reinforce a weak part of a building.

- **Story: Overcoming Negative Thoughts**: David, who struggled with negative self-talk, used CBT techniques to challenge and change his thought patterns. This cognitive restructuring improved his emotional resilience and overall mental health.
3. **Emotional Intelligence (EI) Theory**
    - **Developing EI Components**: Daniel Goleman's Emotional Intelligence framework emphasizes self-awareness, self-regulation, motivation, empathy, and social skills. Developing these components is akin to following a detailed engineering blueprint.
    - **Example: Leadership Training**: In leadership training programs, focusing on EI development has been shown to significantly enhance leaders' effectiveness, team cohesion, and organizational success.

ENGAGING STORIES OF EMOTIONAL ENGINEERING

1. **The Resilient Entrepreneur**
    - **Story of Lisa**: Lisa, an entrepreneur, faced multiple setbacks in her startup journey. By treating each challenge as an engineering problem, she used resilience-building techniques like networking, seeking mentorship, and maintaining a positive mindset. Her emotional skyscraper, although tested by storms, stood tall and robust, leading her to eventual success.
2. **The Compassionate Caregiver**
    - **Story of Mark**: Mark, a nurse in a bustling hospital, often felt overwhelmed by the emotional toll of his job. By using tools like mindfulness, empathy exercises, and maintaining a gratitude journal, he transformed his approach. Mark became known for his calm demeanor

and compassionate care, embodying the principles of emotional engineering in his daily life.
3. **The Balanced Student**
   - **Story of Jenny**: Jenny, a university student, juggled multiple responsibilities. She struggled with stress and burnout until she discovered the concept of emotional engineering. Implementing techniques like time management, self-care routines, and positive affirmations, she built a strong emotional foundation, leading to better academic performance and personal fulfillment.

CONCLUSION: THE SKYSCRAPER OF EMOTIONAL RESILIENCE

As an emotional engineer, you have the tools and blueprint to build a skyscraper of resilience that can withstand life's inevitable challenges. By understanding and managing your emotions, building emotional intelligence, and employing stress management strategies, you can create a robust and adaptable emotional structure. Embrace the role of the emotional engineer, and construct a life of strength, stability, and enduring happiness.

UNDERSTANDING AND MANAGING EMOTIONS

The Great Emotional Rollercoaster

Emotions are like rollercoasters. They're thrilling, scary, and sometimes you just want to throw up. But what if I told you that you could become the rollercoaster engineer, controlling the ups and downs?

Emotional Engineer–Designing Emotional Resilience 79

BECOMING THE ROLLERCOASTER ENGINEER

Identify Your Emotions: Naming the Passengers

1. **Identify Your Emotions**
   - **Start with Self-Reflection**: Spend a few moments each day reflecting on your emotional state. Ask yourself questions like, 'What am I feeling right now?' or 'What triggered this emotion?'
   - **Emotional Vocabulary**: Build a rich vocabulary to describe your emotions. Instead of just feeling 'bad,' try 'disappointed,' 'frustrated,' or 'anxious.' The more precisely you can identify your feelings, the better you can manage them.
   - **Tools for Identification**: Use tools like mood journals or emotion charts to track your feelings. Apps like Daylio or Moodfit can help you monitor your emotional trends over time.

Example: Sarah used to feel overwhelmed at work but couldn't pinpoint why. She started keeping an emotion journal, jotting down her feelings throughout the day. Over time, she noticed patterns and realized that her anxiety peaked during meetings. This awareness was the first step towards managing her stress.

ACCEPT YOUR EMOTIONS: EMBRACING THE RIDE

2. **Accept Your Emotions**
   - **Normalize Your Feelings**: Understand that it's okay to feel a wide range of emotions. Emotions are a natural response to life's events.
   - **Self-Compassion**: Practice self-compassion. Be kind to yourself when you experience negative emotions. Instead

of criticizing yourself, acknowledge that it's part of being human.
- **Mindfulness Practices**: Engage in mindfulness practices to observe your emotions without judgement. Techniques like meditation or deep breathing can help you stay present with your feelings.

Example: Tom struggled with anger whenever he faced criticism. By practicing mindfulness, he learned to observe his anger without immediately reacting. This acceptance allowed him to respond more calmly and constructively.

EXPRESS YOUR EMOTIONS: RELEASING THE PRESSURE

3. **Express Your Emotions**
   - **Healthy Outlets**: Find healthy ways to express your emotions. This could be through physical activities like running or yoga, creative outlets like painting or writing, or verbal expressions like talking to a friend.
   - **Communication Skills**: Develop your communication skills to express your emotions clearly and assertively. Use 'I' statements, like 'I feel upset when…' to convey your feelings without blaming others.
   - **Therapeutic Techniques**: Consider therapeutic techniques such as journaling, art therapy, or counseling to explore and express deeper emotions.

Example: Jane found herself bottling up stress, leading to frequent outbursts. She started a daily journaling practice, pouring her thoughts and feelings onto paper. This act of expression helped her manage her stress more effectively and reduced her outbursts.

THEORIES AND INSIGHTS ON EMOTIONAL MANAGEMENT

Emotional Intelligence (EI)

- **Components of EI**: Daniel Goleman's theory of Emotional Intelligence emphasizes self-awareness, self-regulation, motivation, empathy, and social skills. Developing these areas can significantly enhance emotional management.
- **Application**: By focusing on these components, individuals can better understand and manage their emotions, leading to improved personal and professional relationships.

Example: In a corporate setting, training programs that incorporate EI principles have been shown to reduce workplace stress and improve team dynamics.

COGNITIVE BEHAVIORAL THERAPY (CBT)

- **Principles of CBT**: CBT focuses on changing negative thought patterns to alter emotional responses. By identifying and challenging distorted thinking, individuals can manage their emotions more effectively.
- **Techniques**: Techniques like cognitive restructuring, exposure therapy, and stress inoculation are commonly used in CBT to help individuals cope with their emotions.

Example: David, who struggled with social anxiety, used CBT techniques to challenge his negative beliefs about social interactions. This practice helped him reduce his anxiety and become more confident in social settings.

ENGAGING STORIES OF EMOTIONAL MANAGEMENT

The Journey of Emotional Mastery: A Personal Tale

1. **The Story of Emily**: Emily, a young professional, often felt overwhelmed by her emotions. She would swing from joy to despair within hours, leaving her exhausted. Determined to gain control, Emily embarked on a journey of emotional mastery. She started by identifying her emotions, using a mood journal to track her daily feelings. This practice helped her recognize that her emotional swings were often triggered by specific events or interactions.
2. **Acceptance and Mindfulness**: Emily then moved to acceptance. She practiced mindfulness meditation daily, learning to observe her emotions without judgement. This new perspective allowed her to accept her feelings rather than fight them, reducing her overall stress.
3. **Expressing Emotions Creatively**: To express her emotions, Emily took up painting. Each canvas became a reflection of her emotional state, allowing her to release pent-up feelings in a healthy and creative way. She also found solace in sharing her paintings and the stories behind them with friends, fostering deeper connections.

A CORPORATE TRANSFORMATION: EMOTIONAL MANAGEMENT IN THE WORKPLACE

1. **The Case of the Stressed-Out Team**: At a tech startup, the team was constantly stressed and on edge, leading to high turnover and low productivity. The management decided to invest in emotional intelligence training for the entire staff.
2. **Training and Implementation**: The training focused on identifying emotions, practicing self-compassion, and

expressing feelings constructively. Employees learned to communicate more openly, using 'I' statements to express their needs and concerns without creating conflict.
3. **Results**: Over time, the workplace culture transformed. The team became more cohesive, with employees feeling heard and understood. Productivity soared, and turnover rates dropped significantly. The investment in emotional management paid off, creating a more positive and productive work environment.

PRACTICAL STEPS FOR MANAGING EMOTIONS

1. **Daily Reflection**: Spend a few minutes each day reflecting on your emotions. Use prompts like 'What did I feel today?' and 'What triggered these feelings?' to gain insights into your emotional patterns.
2. **Mindfulness Practices**: Incorporate mindfulness into your daily routine. Apps like Headspace or Calm can guide you through meditation sessions to help you stay present with your emotions.
3. **Journaling**: Keep a journal to express your thoughts and feelings. Write freely about your experiences and how they made you feel. This practice can help you process emotions and gain clarity.
4. **Physical Activity**: Engage in regular physical activity to manage stress and improve your mood. Activities like running, yoga, or dancing can be effective outlets for emotional release.
5. **Creative Outlets**: Explore creative outlets such as painting, writing, or playing an instrument. These activities provide a way to express emotions constructively.
6. **Therapy and Counseling**: Seek professional help if you

struggle to manage your emotions. Therapists can provide valuable tools and techniques to help you navigate emotional challenges.

FINAL THOUGHTS: MASTERING THE EMOTIONAL ROLLERCOASTER

Understanding and managing emotions is a journey, much like mastering the controls of a rollercoaster. By identifying, accepting, and expressing your emotions, you can take control of your emotional ride, transforming it from a chaotic experience into a smooth and empowering journey. Embrace the role of the emotional engineer and build a resilient emotional framework that can withstand life's ups and downs with grace and strength.

BUILDING EMOTIONAL INTELLIGENCE

The Emotionally Intelligent Superhero

Think of yourself as an emotional superhero, your cape flapping in the wind. But instead of super strength, your power is emotional intelligence.

1. **Self-Awareness**: Know thyself. Like a superhero discovering their powers, understand your strengths and weaknesses. Keep an emotion diary; it's like your superhero training log.
2. **Self-Regulation**: Keep your cool. Imagine you're a Zen master who's also a ninja. When you're about to explode, take a deep breath, count to ten, or meditate. Control, you must learn.
3. **Motivation**: Find your why. Why do you want to be emotionally intelligent? Maybe it's to have better relationships

or to be the calmest person in a crisis. Whatever it is, let it drive you.
4. **Empathy**: Walk in others' shoes. No, not literally (unless they have really nice shoes), but try to understand their feelings. It's like having a superpower that connects you to others.
5. **Social Skills**: Be the life of the party (even if it's a pity party). Use your emotional intelligence to build strong relationships, resolve conflicts, and be the emotional glue that holds your social circle together.

STRATEGIES FOR STRESS MANAGEMENT

Stress Management: The Emotional Spa Day

Imagine turning your mind into a luxurious spa. Soft music, lavender scents, and a stress-free zone.

1. **Mindfulness and Meditation**: Be present, like a cat staring at a sunbeam. Practice mindfulness to bring your mind to the here and now. Meditation apps can be your new best friend.
2. **Exercise**: Sweat it out. Physical activity releases endorphins, the body's natural stress relievers. It's like giving your emotions a workout and a sauna session all in one.
3. **Time Management**: Get organized. Create a schedule that includes downtime. Prioritize tasks and say no to unnecessary stressors. It's like decluttering your emotional closet.
4. **Healthy Habits**: Eat, sleep, and repeat. Maintain a balanced diet and get enough sleep. Your body and mind are like a car – they need the right fuel and maintenance to run smoothly.
5. **Hobbies**: Do what you love. Engage in activities that bring

> *Emotions are the colors of the soul; they are spectacular and incredible. When you don't feel, the world becomes dull and colorless.*
>
> —William Paul Young

REAL-LIFE EXAMPLES

Meet Jane, the Emotional Architect. Once prone to emotional meltdowns over spilled milk (literally), Jane now navigates life's challenges with the grace of a ballet dancer. She used mindfulness to stay present, practiced empathy to understand her co-workers, and took up pottery as her stress-relief hobby. Now, Jane is the go-to person in her office for conflict resolution and emotional support.

EXERCISES AND ACTIVITIES

Emotion Diary: Blueprint of Your Emotional Landscape

1. **Emotion Diary**
    - **Daily Emotional Check-In**: Start each day by noting your initial emotions upon waking. Are you feeling anxious, excited, or perhaps indifferent? Recognize the subtle shifts in your emotional state throughout the day.
    - **Detailed Entries**: When documenting your emotions, go beyond the surface. Write about the situations that triggered your feelings, your initial reactions, and the aftermath. Include how long the emotion lasted and its intensity.

you joy and relaxation. Whether it's painting, gardening, or playing the ukulele, find your happy place.

- **Reflective Questions**: End each entry with reflective questions like 'What could I have done differently?' or 'What did I learn from this emotional experience?'

Example: Maria, a high school teacher, found herself frequently stressed and unable to pinpoint the reasons. She started an emotion diary and noticed that her stress peaked during parent-teacher conferences. Reflecting on this, she realized that her anxiety stemmed from a fear of judgement. This insight allowed her to prepare better and manage her stress during future meetings.

MINDFULNESS MEDITATION: CULTIVATING INNER PEACE

2. **Mindfulness Meditation**
   - **Structured Practice**: Dedicate a specific time each day for meditation. It could be in the morning to start your day with calm or in the evening to wind down. Consistency is key.
   - **Breath Focus**: Begin by focusing on your breath. Notice the sensation of air entering and leaving your nostrils. If your mind wanders, gently bring your focus back to your breath.
   - **Body Scan**: Occasionally, try a body scan meditation. Mentally scan your body from head to toe, noting any areas of tension or discomfort and consciously relaxing those areas.
   - **Guided Meditation**: Use apps like Insight Timer or Calm for guided meditation sessions. These can provide structure and support, especially for beginners.

Example: John, a busy executive, started feeling overwhelmed by his workload. He incorporated a 10-minute mindfulness meditation into his morning routine. This practice helped him start his day with clarity and focus, significantly reducing his stress levels throughout the day.

GRATITUDE LIST: PLANTING FLOWERS IN THE GARDEN OF YOUR MIND

3. **Gratitude List**
   - **Evening Routine**: Every evening, take a few minutes to write down three things you are grateful for. They can be as simple as a beautiful sunset or as significant as a promotion at work.
   - **Specificity and Variety**: Be specific about what you're grateful for and try to include different things each day. This helps in broadening your perspective and deepening your appreciation.
   - **Reflect on Positive Changes**: Occasionally, look back at your gratitude lists to reflect on how your outlook has changed over time. Notice if there are recurring themes and what they reveal about your values and priorities.

Example: Emily, who often felt overwhelmed by negative thoughts, started keeping a gratitude journal. Over time, she noticed a shift in her perspective, focusing more on the positive aspects of her life. This practice improved her overall happiness and helped her deal with daily challenges more effectively.

ADDITIONAL EXERCISES AND ACTIVITIES FOR EMOTIONAL MASTERY

Visualization: Creating a Mental Sanctuary

4. **Visualization**
   - **Create a Mental Sanctuary**: Visualize a place where you feel completely at peace. It could be a beach, a forest, or a cozy room. Spend a few minutes each day imagining yourself in this sanctuary, soaking in the calm and serenity.
   - **Positive Outcomes**: Visualize positive outcomes for situations that cause you anxiety. Imagine yourself handling them with confidence and ease.

Example: Lisa, who often felt nervous before presentations, used visualization to imagine herself speaking confidently and engagingly. This mental rehearsal helped her reduce anxiety and perform better during actual presentations.

PROGRESSIVE MUSCLE RELAXATION: EASING PHYSICAL TENSION

5. **Progressive Muscle Relaxation (PMR)**
   - **Step-by-Step Relaxation**: PMR involves tensing and then relaxing different muscle groups in your body. Start from your toes and work your way up to your head.
   - **Regular Practice**: Practice PMR regularly, especially during times of high stress, to help your body recognize and release tension.

Example: Mark, a college student, used PMR to manage his exam stress. By regularly practicing PMR, he was able to stay calm and focused during exams, improving his performance.

COGNITIVE RESTRUCTURING: CHANGING THOUGHT PATTERNS

6. **Cognitive Restructuring**
   - **Identify Negative Thoughts**: Notice when you have negative or irrational thoughts. Write them down.
   - **Challenge and Replace**: Challenge these thoughts by asking questions like 'Is this really true?' or 'What evidence do I have?' Replace them with more balanced and positive thoughts.

Example: David often felt like a failure whenever he faced setbacks. By practicing cognitive restructuring, he learned to challenge these negative thoughts and replace them with more constructive ones, such as recognizing his efforts and potential for growth.

ACTIVE LISTENING: ENHANCING EMPATHY AND CONNECTION

7. **Active Listening**
   - **Fully Engage**: When listening to someone, give them your full attention. Avoid interrupting or planning your response while they are speaking.
   - **Reflect and Clarify**: Reflect back what you've heard and ask clarifying questions to ensure you understand their perspective.

Example: Jane, who struggled with her relationships, started practicing active listening. This improved her empathy and understanding, leading to stronger and more meaningful connections with others.

THEORIES AND INSIGHTS ON EMOTIONAL EXERCISES

Self-Determination Theory (SDT)

- **Intrinsic Motivation**: SDT emphasizes the importance of intrinsic motivation and personal growth. Exercises like mindfulness and gratitude align with SDT by fostering a sense of autonomy, competence, and relatedness.
- **Application**: By engaging in activities that resonate personally, individuals can enhance their emotional well-being and overall satisfaction.

Example: By choosing to practice mindfulness and gratitude out of personal interest rather than external pressure, individuals can experience greater motivation and fulfillment.

POSITIVE PSYCHOLOGY

- **Focus on Strengths**: Positive psychology encourages focusing on strengths and positive aspects of life. Exercises like gratitude lists and visualization are rooted in this theory, promoting a positive mindset and resilience.
- **Application**: Incorporating positive psychology principles can help individuals build a more optimistic and resilient outlook on life.

Example: Sarah, who often felt overwhelmed by challenges, found that focusing on her strengths and positive experiences helped her build resilience and cope more effectively with stress.

ENGAGING STORIES OF EMOTIONAL EXERCISES

The Transformative Power of Journaling

1. **Story of Alex**: Alex, a college student, felt lost and disconnected from his emotions. He started an emotion diary, detailing his feelings and experiences each day. This practice helped him uncover patterns in his emotions and understand their triggers. Over time, Alex felt more in control of his emotional landscape and was able to navigate college life with greater ease and confidence.

MINDFULNESS IN THE MIDST OF CHAOS

2. **Story of Rachel**: Rachel, a nurse working in a high-stress environment, struggled with burnout. She incorporated mindfulness meditation into her daily routine, taking 10 minutes each day to focus on her breath and center herself. This practice became her anchor amidst the chaos, helping her stay calm and composed, ultimately improving her performance and well-being.

GRATITUDE AS A LIFELINE

3. **Story of Michael**: Michael, who faced a series of personal setbacks, felt overwhelmed by negativity. He started writing a daily gratitude list, focusing on the small joys in his life. This practice helped him shift his perspective, fostering a sense of hope and resilience that carried him through difficult times.

PRACTICAL STEPS FOR IMPLEMENTING EMOTIONAL EXERCISES

1. **Set a Routine**: Establish a daily routine for your emotional exercises. Consistency is key to reaping the benefits.
2. **Create a Dedicated Space**: Find a quiet, comfortable space where you can practice mindfulness, journaling, and other exercises without distractions.
3. **Use Technology**: Leverage technology, such as apps and online resources, to guide your practices and track your progress.
4. **Seek Support**: Join a community or find a buddy to share your journey with. Mutual support can enhance motivation and accountability.
5. **Be Patient**: Emotional mastery is a gradual process. Be patient with yourself and celebrate small victories along the way.

FINAL THOUGHTS: BUILDING EMOTIONAL MASTERY THROUGH PRACTICE

Exercises and activities like emotion diaries, mindfulness meditation, and gratitude lists are powerful tools for developing emotional mastery. By integrating these practices into your daily life, you can build a resilient and positive emotional framework. Embrace the journey, and watch as your emotional landscape transforms, bringing greater peace, clarity, and fulfillment into your life.

BRIEF: THE JOURNEY OF EMOTIONAL ENGINEERING

Emotional engineering is not just a skill but an art form, a dynamic process that encompasses understanding and managing your emotions, building emotional intelligence, and employing effective strategies for stress management. This chapter has taken you on a journey of self-discovery, resilience, and continuous growth, highlighting the importance of embracing your inner emotional superhero and transforming your emotional rollercoaster into a smooth and thrilling ride.

UNDERSTANDING AND MANAGING YOUR EMOTIONS: THE CORE OF EMOTIONAL ENGINEERING

Understanding and managing your emotions is the foundational pillar of emotional engineering. It's about recognizing your feelings, accepting them without judgement, and finding healthy ways to express them.

1. **Identifying Emotions**: The first step in managing your emotions is identifying them accurately. Emotions are complex and multi-faceted, often intertwining with one another. Developing an emotional vocabulary and keeping an emotion diary helps in pinpointing specific emotions and their triggers.
   Example: Imagine Sarah, who always felt anxious during team meetings. By keeping an emotion diary, she realized that her anxiety was linked to a fear of public speaking. Identifying this allowed her to work on her presentation skills, gradually reducing her anxiety.
2. **Accepting Emotions**: Acceptance is about acknowledging your emotions without trying to suppress or deny them. It's understanding that emotions are a natural part of being human.
   Example: Tom, who frequently felt anger when criticized, learned to accept his anger as a valid emotion. By practicing

mindfulness, he could observe his anger without letting it control his reactions, leading to more constructive responses.
3. **Expressing Emotions**: Finding healthy outlets for your emotions is crucial. Whether it's through talking to a friend, engaging in physical activity, or creative pursuits like painting or writing, expressing emotions helps release pent-up feelings.
Example: Jane, who bottled up her stress, started journaling her thoughts and feelings. This simple act of expression helped her manage her stress better and improved her overall well-being.

BUILDING EMOTIONAL INTELLIGENCE: THE FRAMEWORK OF EMOTIONAL ENGINEERING

Building emotional intelligence involves developing self-awareness, self-regulation, motivation, empathy, and social skills. These components work together to create a robust framework for emotional resilience and effective interpersonal relationships.

1. **Self-Awareness**: Knowing yourself is the cornerstone of emotional intelligence. It's about recognizing your emotions and understanding their impact on your thoughts and behaviors.
   Example: David, a manager, realized that his frustration with his team was affecting his leadership. By becoming more self-aware, he learned to manage his frustration and communicate more effectively, improving team dynamics.
2. **Self-Regulation**: This involves managing your emotions, especially in stressful situations, and maintaining control over your impulses.
   Example: Mio, a teacher, practiced deep breathing exercises before entering her classroom each morning. This helped

her remain calm and composed, even when dealing with challenging students.

3. **Motivation**: Intrinsic motivation drives you to pursue goals with passion and perseverance, even in the face of setbacks.
   Example: Michael, a sales representative, faced numerous rejections. However, his intrinsic motivation to succeed kept him pushing forward, eventually leading to significant achievements in his career.

4. **Empathy**: Understanding and sharing the feelings of others is key to building strong relationships.
   Example: Emily, a nurse, developed her empathy skills by actively listening to her patients' concerns. This not only improved patient satisfaction but also made her more effective in her role.

5. **Social Skills**: Effective communication, conflict resolution, and building strong relationships are essential social skills.
   Example: John, who struggled with workplace conflicts, attended a workshop on conflict resolution. He learned techniques to manage disputes constructively, which improved the overall work environment.

EMPLOYING STRATEGIES FOR STRESS MANAGEMENT: THE TOOLS OF EMOTIONAL ENGINEERING

Stress management is crucial in emotional engineering. It involves employing various strategies to cope with stress and maintain emotional balance.

1. **Mindfulness and Meditation**: Regular mindfulness practices help reduce stress by keeping you grounded in the present moment.
   Example: Rachel, a high-stress executive, started a daily mindfulness meditation routine. This practice helped her

manage stress and improved her decision-making abilities.
2. **Physical Activity**: Exercise is a powerful stress reliever, releasing endorphins that boost your mood.
   Example: Mark, who faced chronic stress, incorporated running into his daily routine. This not only improved his physical health but also significantly reduced his stress levels.
3. **Healthy Lifestyle Choices**: Maintaining a balanced diet, getting enough sleep, and avoiding harmful habits contribute to overall well-being.
   Example: Jenny, who often felt fatigued and stressed, made a commitment to improve her diet and sleep patterns. This holistic approach improved her energy levels and emotional stability.
4. **Time Management**: Prioritizing tasks and managing time effectively can reduce stress and increase productivity.
   Example: Alex, a college student, felt overwhelmed by his coursework. By creating a detailed study schedule and sticking to it, he managed his time better and reduced his stress.
5. **Seeking Support**: Sometimes, talking to a friend, mentor, or therapist can provide the support you need to manage stress.
   Example: Maria, who struggled with work-life balance, sought guidance from a mentor. This support helped her navigate her challenges and find a healthier balance.

THEORIES AND INSIGHTS IN EMOTIONAL ENGINEERING

1. **Maslow's Hierarchy of Needs**: This theory emphasizes the importance of fulfilling basic needs before achieving self-

actualization. Emotional well-being is tied to meeting these needs.

Application: By ensuring basic needs like safety and belonging are met, individuals can focus on higher-level emotional development.

2. **Cognitive Behavioral Therapy (CBT)**: CBT helps in changing negative thought patterns that contribute to emotional distress.

   Example: Sarah used CBT techniques to challenge her negative thoughts about public speaking, replacing them with positive affirmations, which helped her manage her anxiety.

3. **Positive Psychology**: This field focuses on strengths and positive aspects of life, promoting resilience and well-being.

   Example: Michael, who practiced gratitude, found that focusing on positive experiences significantly improved his emotional resilience.

ENGAGING STORIES OF EMOTIONAL ENGINEERING

The Resilient Entrepreneur

1. **Story of Maya:** Maya, a small business owner, encountered numerous setbacks in her entrepreneurial journey. Rather than surrendering to defeat, she embraced every failure as a lesson. By adopting stress-relief meditation and regular yoga, Maya built a strong sense of resilience. Her determination bore fruit when she eventually launched a thriving business, inspiring many.

THE COMPASSIONATE CAREGIVER

2. **Story of Mark**: Mark, a caregiver, often felt overwhelmed by the emotional demands of his job. He began practicing

mindfulness meditation and journaling his experiences. These activities helped him process his emotions and maintain a positive outlook. Mark's compassionate care and emotional resilience not only benefited his patients but also inspired his colleagues.

THE BALANCED STUDENT

3. **Story of Jenny**: Jenny, a university student, struggled with the pressures of academics and extracurricular activities. She started using time management strategies, mindfulness practices, and sought support from a counselor. These efforts helped her find balance and excel both academically and personally. Jenny's journey of emotional engineering made her a more resilient and well-rounded individual.

FINAL THOUGHTS: EMBRACING YOUR INNER EMOTIONAL SUPERHERO

Emotional engineering is a comprehensive approach to mastering your emotions, building emotional intelligence, and managing stress effectively. It's a continuous journey of self-discovery and growth, requiring dedication and practice. By embracing your inner emotional superhero, you can transform your emotional rollercoaster into a smooth and thrilling ride, achieving a balanced and fulfilling life.

6

Relationship Architect–Building Strong Connections

WELCOME TO THE RELATIONSHIP ARCHITECT'S WORKSHOP!

Imagine you're building a skyscraper in the middle of a bustling city. Now, would you ever consider constructing this without a solid foundation and support beams? No way! The same applies to your relationships. Whether it's family, friends, or that barista who knows exactly how you like your coffee, everyone needs a strong support network.

1. The Foundation of Emotional Stability

Support networks are like the WiFi of life – invisible but absolutely essential. Without them, you're stuck buffering, and let's be honest, nobody likes buffering. These networks provide emotional support, practical assistance, and sometimes just someone to share memes with. They're the people who lift you up, even when you've had one of those days where nothing goes right, and you've just discovered you've been wearing your shirt inside out since morning.

Example: The Lifeline of Friends

Think of Emma, a college student away from home for the first time. The transition is tough, and she feels the weight of homesickness. Her new friends become her lifeline. They study together, share meals, and explore the campus. One night, after a particularly rough day, Emma finds solace in her friend's dorm, sharing her worries over a tub of ice cream. This emotional support is her anchor, keeping her grounded and resilient.

2. Practical Assistance in Times of Need

Beyond emotional support, a robust network provides practical help. Whether it's moving to a new apartment, needing a ride to the airport, or just borrowing a cup of sugar, these small acts of kindness are the glue that binds relationships.

Example: The Moving Day Miracle

Consider Jake, who is relocating to a new city for work. He's overwhelmed with packing, organizing, and the logistics of the move. Enter his support network: friends who show up with boxes, tape, and a ready attitude. One friend even offers to drive the moving truck. What could have been a stressful ordeal turns into a day filled with laughter, pizza breaks, and teamwork. Jake realizes that without his support network, this transition would have been daunting.

3. Shared Interests and Activities

Support networks also form around shared interests and activities, which enrich our lives with joy and purpose. Hobbies, sports, and shared passions create bonds that go beyond superficial interactions.

Example: The Book Club Bond

Lena loves reading but finds it a solitary activity until she joins a local book club. Here, she meets diverse people who share her passion for literature. They discuss themes, argue over character motives, and even embark on literary-themed outings. This community not only expands her understanding of books but also deepens her connection with others who appreciate the same things she does.

4. Professional and Personal Growth

A strong support network can be a catalyst for growth. Mentors, colleagues, and peers provide invaluable advice, feedback, and opportunities. They challenge us, celebrate our successes, and help us navigate professional landscapes.

Example: The Mentor's Wisdom

Imagine Sarah, an ambitious young professional navigating the corporate world. Her mentor, with years of experience, becomes her guide. They meet regularly, discussing career strategies, leadership skills, and personal development. When Sarah faces a major project, her mentor's advice is crucial. She not only succeeds but gains confidence and insight. This professional support network propels her career forward.

5. Coping with Life's Challenges

Life is unpredictable, and everyone faces challenges. During tough times, a support network acts as a safety net, providing strength and resources to cope with adversity.

Example: The Unexpected Crisis

Tom's life takes a sudden turn when he loses his job. He feels lost and anxious about the future. His support network, comprising family and friends, rallies around him. They offer financial help, job leads, and emotional support. His best friend even helps him revamp his resume. Through their collective efforts, Tom lands a new job and feels more connected and valued than ever.

6. Creating a Sense of Belonging

Support networks create a sense of belonging, which is crucial for mental health. Feeling accepted and understood reduces feelings of loneliness and isolation.

Example: The Community Connection

Alicia moves to a new town where she knows no one. She joins a local running club and quickly finds her place. The shared early morning runs, encouragement during races, and post-run breakfasts forge strong bonds. She no longer feels like an outsider but a valued member of the community.

7. Theoretical Perspectives on Support Networks

From a psychological perspective, Maslow's Hierarchy of Needs highlights the importance of love and belonging as fundamental human needs. Similarly, Social Support Theory emphasizes that social relationships improve mental and physical health by providing emotional, instrumental, informational, and appraisal support.

Engaging Story: The Marathon of Support

Consider David, training for his first marathon. His journey is fraught with challenges – physical exhaustion, mental strain, and self-doubt. However, his support network makes all the difference. His running buddy keeps him motivated during early morning runs. His family cheers him on at every milestone. His online running group offers tips and encouragement. On race day, he crosses the finish line not just with personal triumph but with the collective strength of his support network.

8. Building and Maintaining Support Networks

Creating a support network requires effort, reciprocity, and genuine connections. It's about being there for others as much as they are for you.

Example: The Reciprocity Rule

Maya often helps her neighbor, Mrs. Green, with groceries. One winter, Maya falls ill, and Mrs. Green brings over homemade soup and offers to walk Maya's dog. This reciprocal relationship strengthens their bond, showing that support is a two-way street.

9. Expanding Your Network

Don't limit your support network to just a few close friends or family. Expand it by joining clubs, volunteering, and participating in community events.

Example: The Volunteer's Reward

John volunteers at a local animal shelter. Through this, he meets people who share his love for animals. They not only bond over their furry friends but also form a network that supports each other in various aspects of life – from job referrals to house-sitting pets. This expanded network enriches John's life in unexpected ways.

10. The Digital Age of Support

In today's digital age, support networks extend beyond geographical boundaries. Online communities, social media groups, and virtual meetings create new avenues for support.

Example: The Global Village

Ravi, a tech enthusiast, joins an online forum for coders. Here, he finds a mentor from Australia, collaborates on projects with peers from Canada, and gets feedback from experts around the world. This digital support network accelerates his learning and broadens his horizons, proving that distance is no barrier to meaningful connections.

Support networks are the bedrock of a fulfilling life. They provide emotional, practical, and professional support, helping us navigate the complexities of existence. By investing in and nurturing these networks, we not only enrich our own lives but also contribute to a more connected and compassionate world. So, go ahead, be a Relationship Architect, and build those strong, resilient connections that will stand the test of time. And remember, just like a skyscraper, your support network needs regular maintenance – cherish it, nurture it, and it will stand tall through all of life's ups and downs.

COMMUNICATION SKILLS FOR DEEPER RELATIONSHIPS

Talk the Talk, Walk the Walk

Communication skills are the Swiss Army knife of relationships. You need them for everything – resolving conflicts, expressing love, and even for deciding who gets the last slice of pizza (always a critical decision). Good communication can turn a potential disaster into a minor hiccup. Imagine arguing over who left the milk out overnight but resolving it with a laugh rather than a cold war.

PRO TIPS FOR EFFECTIVE COMMUNICATION

1. Listen Like a Therapist

Active listening is the cornerstone of effective communication. When you listen attentively, you show the other person that you value their words and feelings.

Example: The Listening Partner Imagine a couple, Sarah and Jake. Jake is frustrated after a tough day at work. Instead of interrupting or offering solutions immediately, Sarah practices active listening. She nods, maintains eye contact, and occasionally says, 'I understand.' Jake feels heard and appreciated, which diffuses his frustration and strengthens their bond.

Theory: Carl Rogers' Active Listening Carl Rogers, a renowned psychologist, emphasized the importance of active listening in building effective communication. He believed that listening empathetically allows individuals to express their thoughts and emotions freely, leading to better understanding and stronger relationships.

2. Use 'I' Statements

Using 'I' statements helps in expressing your feelings without sounding accusatory. It shifts the focus from blaming the other person to sharing your own experience.

Example: The Dish Dilemma Consider this scenario: Laura and Tom often argue about household chores. Instead of saying, 'You never help with the dishes,' Laura tries, 'I feel overwhelmed when the dishes pile up.' This approach opens a space for dialogue rather than defensiveness.

Theory: Nonviolent Communication by Marshall Rosenberg
Marshall Rosenberg's Nonviolent Communication (NVC) framework highlights the use of 'I' statements to express needs and feelings without blaming others. This method fosters empathy and mutual understanding.

3. Humor It Up

Laughter is a powerful tool in communication. It breaks tension and brings people closer together.

Example: The Forgotten Anniversary Anna forgets her anniversary, and her partner, Mike, is initially upset. Instead of sulking, Mike lightens the mood with a joke: 'I guess we'll just have to celebrate twice as hard next year!' They both laugh, turning a potential conflict into a shared moment of joy.

Theory: Humor in Relationships Studies have shown that couples who use humor to resolve conflicts are more likely to have long-lasting and satisfying relationships. Humor can reduce stress, increase positivity, and enhance emotional connection.

EXPANDING COMMUNICATION TECHNIQUES

4. Clarify and Confirm

Misunderstandings often occur when assumptions are made. Clarifying and confirming ensures that both parties are on the same page.

Example: The Mixed Message John tells Maria he will be late for dinner. Maria assumes he means an hour late, but John arrives three hours later, leading to frustration. By clarifying,

'I'll be home around 9 PM,' John could have avoided the misunderstanding.

Theory: The Ladder of Inference by Chris Argyris The Ladder of Inference explains how people move from facts to assumptions and actions. Clarifying and confirming steps help ensure that interpretations are aligned with reality, preventing miscommunications.

5. Nonverbal Communication

Nonverbal cues, such as body language, facial expressions, and tone of voice, play a crucial role in communication. They often convey more than words.

Example: The Silent Signal During a heated discussion, Rachel crosses her arms and looks away. David notices her body language and says, 'I see you're upset. Can we take a break and talk later?' Recognizing nonverbal signals helps address underlying emotions.

Theory: Mehrabian's Communication Model Albert Mehrabian's model suggests that 93% of communication is nonverbal (55% body language, 38% tone of voice). Understanding and using nonverbal cues can enhance communication effectiveness.

6. Empathy and Validation

Empathy involves understanding and sharing the feelings of others. Validation acknowledges their emotions, making them feel respected and understood.

Example: The Empathetic Friend Julie shares her worries about a job interview with her friend Sam. Instead of dismissing her fears, Sam says, 'I can see why you're nervous. Job interviews can be really stressful.' This validation makes Julie feel supported and understood.

Theory: Emotional Intelligence by Daniel Goleman Emotional intelligence, as explained by Daniel Goleman, includes empathy as a key component. Empathy and validation are essential for building deep and meaningful relationships.

7. Open-Ended Questions

Asking open-ended questions encourages dialogue and deeper understanding. These questions require more than a yes or no answer, promoting thoughtful responses.

Example: The Dinner Conversation Instead of asking, 'Did you have a good day?' which can be answered with a simple yes or no, ask, 'What was the highlight of your day?' This invites the other person to share more about their experiences.

Theory: The Art of Asking Questions Open-ended questions foster meaningful conversations by encouraging elaboration and exploration. They show genuine interest and facilitate deeper connections.

ENGAGING STORIES: THE POWER OF COMMUNICATION

Story 1: The Lost Keys

Lucy and Mark often argue about misplaced items. One day, Lucy loses her keys and Mark, instead of getting angry, asks calmly, 'Where did you last see them?' Together, they retrace her steps and find the keys. This cooperative approach, driven by good communication, prevents a potential argument.

Story 2: The Project Partners

Emma and Jack are working on a project together. Emma feels overwhelmed but doesn't say anything. Jack notices her stress and asks, 'Is everything okay? Do you need help with any part of the project?' Emma feels relieved and shares her concerns. Jack offers his assistance, and they complete the project successfully, strengthening their partnership.

THEORETICAL PERSPECTIVES AND PRACTICAL APPLICATIONS

Theory: The Johari Window

The Johari Window is a communication model that helps individuals understand their relationships with themselves and others. It includes four quadrants: Open, Blind, Hidden, and Unknown. Effective communication enlarges the Open area, fostering transparency and mutual understanding.

Application: Team Building Exercise During a team-building exercise, members share feedback and insights. This practice increases self-awareness and openness, leading to improved team dynamics and communication.

THEORY: TRANSACTIONAL ANALYSIS BY ERIC BERNE

Transactional Analysis (TA) explores interactions (transactions) between people. It identifies three ego states: Parent, Adult, and Child. Effective communication occurs when transactions are complementary (Adult-Adult) rather than crossed (Parent-Child).

Application: Conflict Resolution In a conflict, individuals can use TA to recognize their ego states and shift to Adult-Adult transactions. This approach promotes rational dialogue and problem-solving.

PRACTICAL TIPS FOR EVERYDAY COMMUNICATION

1. Practice Mindfulness
Being present in the moment enhances communication. Mindfulness helps you focus on the conversation, reducing distractions and misunderstandings.

2. Paraphrase and Reflect
Paraphrasing the other person's words shows that you understand and are actively engaged. Reflecting on their emotions further validates their feelings.

3. Avoid Interrupting
Allow the other person to finish their thoughts before responding. Interrupting can lead to frustration and hinder effective communication.

4. Stay Positive
Maintaining a positive tone, even in disagreements, helps keep the conversation constructive and respectful.

Communication is the lifeblood of relationships. By honing your communication skills, you can deepen your connections, resolve conflicts effectively, and express love and appreciation. Whether through active listening, empathetic responses, or a well-timed joke, mastering the art of communication can transform your relationships and enrich your life. So, talk the talk and walk the walk, and watch your relationships thrive.

SETTING BOUNDARIES AND MANAGING TOXICITY

No Toxic Zone – Boundaries in Relationships

Setting boundaries is like putting up fences around your garden. It keeps the good stuff in and the pesky weeds (or toxic people) out. Boundaries ensure that relationships are healthy and that everyone's needs are respected.

UNDERSTANDING BOUNDARIES

1. The Purpose of Boundaries

Boundaries are essential for maintaining healthy relationships and self-respect. They define what is acceptable behavior and what is not, ensuring mutual respect and understanding.

Example: The Personal Space Rule Consider Alice, who values her personal space and time. She sets a boundary with her friend Lucy, explaining that while she loves spending time together, she needs some alone time to recharge. This clear communication prevents misunderstandings and maintains their friendship's health.

Theory: Boundary Theory Boundary Theory suggests that boundaries help individuals manage their relationships by regulating the level of intimacy and closeness. Healthy boundaries allow for balanced connections without feeling overwhelmed or exploited.

MASTERING THE ART OF 'NO'

Learning to say 'no' effectively is a crucial aspect of setting boundaries. It helps protect your time, energy, and well-being without feeling guilty.

2. Politely Decline
Saying 'no' politely but firmly is an art. It ensures that you respect your own needs while being considerate of others' feelings.

Example: The Weekend Planner Imagine Jane, who is often overwhelmed by requests for help. When a colleague asks for assistance over the weekend, she replies, 'I'd love to help, but I've got plans to binge-watch my favorite series all weekend.' This light-hearted yet clear response maintains her boundary without causing offense.

Theory: Politeness Theory by Brown and Levinson Politeness Theory explains that maintaining politeness helps manage social interactions and minimize conflict. Using polite refusals respects the other person's face (self-esteem) while asserting your boundaries.

3. Assertive but Kind
Being assertive means standing up for your needs while remaining kind and respectful. It's about balancing firmness with empathy.

Example: The Me-Time Request Mark feels drained after a busy week. When his friends invite him out, he responds, 'I need some 'me time' to recharge. Let's catch up another day.' This assertive yet kind response ensures his well-being while keeping his friendships intact.

Theory: Assertiveness Training Assertiveness Training teaches individuals how to express their needs and desires confidently and respectfully. It emphasizes the importance of self-advocacy while maintaining positive relationships.

4. Blame the Goldfish
Using humor can diffuse tension and make refusals less confrontational. It adds a light-hearted element to boundary-setting.

Example: The Absurd Excuse Tom's neighbor frequently asks for favors. To avoid constant requests, Tom humorously says, 'I'd love to, but my goldfish has a dentist appointment.' The absurdity of the excuse makes the refusal less harsh and more memorable.

IDENTIFYING AND MANAGING TOXICITY

Toxic relationships are like eating expired sushi – they seem okay at first but soon leave you feeling terrible. Learning to spot the signs of toxicity is crucial for maintaining your mental and emotional health.

5. Spotting Toxic Signs

Identifying toxic behavior early helps you take proactive steps to protect yourself.

Signs to Watch For:

- Constant negativity or criticism.
- Manipulative behavior.
- Lack of respect for your boundaries.

Example: The Criticizing Friend Samantha's friend, Emma, constantly criticizes her choices and undermines her confidence. Recognizing these toxic signs, Samantha decides to set firm boundaries and limit her interactions with Emma to protect her self-esteem.

Theory: Toxic Relationship Indicators Psychological research identifies specific behaviors that signify toxic relationships, such as gaslighting, emotional manipulation, and consistent negativity. Recognizing these indicators helps in managing and mitigating their impact.

DEALING WITH TOXICITY

Managing toxic relationships requires strategic and deliberate actions to safeguard your well-being.

6. Distance is Your Friend

Sometimes, the best way to deal with toxic people is to limit your interactions with them. Creating distance helps reduce their negative impact on your life.

Example: The Distancing Strategy Jake's colleague, Paul, constantly spreads office gossip and negativity. To avoid being affected, Jake minimizes his interactions with Paul and focuses on building positive relationships with other coworkers. This distancing strategy helps Jake maintain a healthier work environment.

Theory: The Law of Reciprocity The Law of Reciprocity suggests that individuals reciprocate the behavior they receive. By distancing yourself from toxic people, you reduce the likelihood of engaging in negative exchanges and promote healthier interactions.

7. Direct Communication

Being honest and clear about what behavior is unacceptable helps address issues directly. The sandwich method – compliment, critique, compliment – can be an effective approach.

Example: The Tardy Friend When addressing his friend's chronic lateness, Mike says, 'You're really fun to hang out with, but I feel hurt when you're always late. I really enjoy our time together when we're both punctual.' This direct communication highlights the issue without being confrontational.

Theory: The Feedback Sandwich The Feedback Sandwich method, commonly used in management and psychology, involves delivering feedback in a way that starts and ends with positive statements, making the critique more palatable and constructive.

STORIES OF BOUNDARIES AND MANAGING TOXICITY

Story 1: The Overbearing Relative

Lisa's aunt, Carol, often drops by unannounced, disrupting Lisa's work-from-home routine. After enduring this for months, Lisa decides to set a boundary. She calls Carol and says, 'Aunt Carol, I love spending time with you, but I need to focus on my work during the day. Can we schedule visits for the weekends?' Carol initially feels offended but eventually respects Lisa's boundary. This clear communication preserves their relationship while ensuring Lisa's productivity.

Story 2: The Manipulative Friend

Alex has a friend, Dave, who often manipulates him into doing favors, making Alex feel guilty if he refuses. Realizing the toxicity, Alex decides to address it. During their next interaction, Alex says, 'Dave, I value our friendship, but I feel taken advantage of when you pressure me into things. I need us to respect each other's time and boundaries.' Dave is taken aback but agrees to be more considerate. This direct approach helps Alex reclaim his autonomy.

THEORETICAL PERSPECTIVES ON BOUNDARIES AND TOXICITY

Theory: Bowen's Family Systems Theory

Bowen's Family Systems Theory suggests that individuals are part of a larger family system, and their behaviors influence and are influenced by other family members. Setting boundaries helps maintain healthy differentiation and prevent enmeshment.

Application: Family Boundaries In a family where members are overly involved in each other's lives, setting boundaries can prevent emotional enmeshment. For instance, Sarah sets a boundary with her parents, explaining that while she values their advice, she needs to make her own decisions. This maintains her independence while preserving family harmony.

THEORY: THE DRAMA TRIANGLE BY STEPHEN KARPMAN

The Drama Triangle identifies three roles in a conflict: Victim, Persecutor, and Rescuer. Understanding these roles helps individuals recognize toxic dynamics and set boundaries to avoid being drawn into unhealthy patterns.

Application: Breaking the Triangle Jenny often finds herself playing the Rescuer in her friends' dramas, feeling drained and unappreciated. Recognizing the pattern, she sets boundaries by refusing to engage in their conflicts and encourages them to solve their issues independently. This shift breaks the cycle and empowers her friends to take responsibility for their actions.

PRACTICAL TIPS FOR SETTING BOUNDARIES

1. Be Consistent
Consistency in enforcing boundaries reinforces their importance. Don't waver or make exceptions that compromise your well-being.

2. Communicate Clearly
Clearly articulate your boundaries. Use direct and specific language to avoid misunderstandings.

3. Use Positive Reinforcement
Acknowledge and appreciate when others respect your boundaries. Positive reinforcement encourages continued respect.

4. Seek Support
If you struggle with setting boundaries, seek support from trusted friends, a therapist, or a support group.

Setting boundaries and managing toxicity are essential for maintaining healthy and fulfilling relationships. By mastering the art of saying 'no,' identifying toxic behavior, and addressing issues directly, you can create a No Toxic Zone in your life. Boundaries ensure that your needs are respected, and your relationships remain positive and supportive. So, go ahead, put up those fences, and enjoy the peace and harmony that come with well-maintained boundaries.

EXERCISES AND ACTIVITIES

Build Your Relationship Toolbox

1. **The Compliment Game**: Spend a week giving genuine compliments to those around you. Notice how it changes the dynamics.
2. **The Listening Challenge**: For one day, practice listening more than you speak. Take mental notes on how it affects your conversations.
3. **The Boundary Exercise**: Identify one area where you need to set a boundary and implement it. Reflect on how it feels and the response from others.

BRIEF

Relationships are the glue that holds our lives together, and like any good glue, they need the right ingredients and application to be effective. Build your support network, communicate like a pro, and set boundaries to keep out the toxicity. And don't forget to sprinkle in a little humor – after all, laughter is the shortest distance between two people.

So, go forth, Relationship Architects, and build those strong, magnificent connections! And remember, even the tallest skyscrapers started with a single brick... or in this case, a single conversation.

> *Success is the sum of small efforts,*
> *repeated day in and day out.*
>
> —Robert Collier

PRACTICAL ASPECTS OF LIFE

Picture embarking on a journey without a map, a chef without a recipe, or a puzzle missing pieces. Just as these scenarios spell chaos, so does your financial life without well-defined objectives. This book is your manual for converting hazy financial aspirations into actionable plans.

Every remarkable adventure starts with a single, clear-cut aim – a lighthouse guiding the traveler through stormy seas and mysterious lands. Similarly, your financial path needs a precise goal, a guiding star to lead you towards monetary stability and success.

ESTABLISHING FINANCIAL GOALS

Defining Your Path

Every trip needs a destination, and every book needs a clear focus. This book's primary mission is to help you comprehend, set, and achieve your financial targets. But what does it mean to establish a financial goal, and why is it so essential?

THE HEART OF FINANCIAL GOALS

Financial goals aren't just figures on a ledger; they symbolize our dreams, ambitions, and hopes. They outline a path to where we want to be and how to get there. These goals can range from short-term aims like saving for a holiday to long-term objectives such as amassing a retirement fund.

EXAMPLE 1: THE DREAM OF HOME OWNERSHIP

Meet Lisa, a young professional with a dream of purchasing her first home. Without a defined financial goal, this dream stays out of reach. By specifying her aim (e.g., saving $50,000 for a down payment within five years), Lisa establishes a concrete target. This goal drives her to budget, save, and invest wisely, making her dream achievable.

REAL-LIFE NARRATIVES: PRACTICAL APPLICATIONS

The Journey of Alex and Sarah

Alex and Sarah, a young couple, noticed that much of their income was slipping away on impulsive takeaways. Determined to change, they set a firm goal: to save £25,000 over the next three years for a new business idea. With this target in mind, they revamped their spending habits, created a strict budget, eliminated unnecessary expenses like eating junk food regularly. Few years later, they not only achieved their savings goal but also developed financial stability that would serve them well in the future.

THE SCIENCE OF GOAL-SETTING

Psychologist Edwin Locke's Goal-Setting Theory stresses the importance of clear, specific goals. According to Locke, goals act as motivators, directing focus and effort towards activities that achieve the goal. Clear goals also boost persistence and encourage the development of strategies to meet them. This theory highlights why defining a clear purpose is crucial for financial success.

Just as Practical Paul realized that his savings wouldn't grow on their own, you need to set clear financial goals to realize your dreams. Begin by envisioning your ideal financial future, jot it down, and break it into manageable steps. Research shows that people with clear, written goals are 42% more likely to achieve them – it's science, not magic!

Through real-life stories, practical examples, and psychological insights, this book offers a thorough approach to financial goal setting. By adhering to these principles, you can turn your vague financial dreams into concrete realities and navigate your financial journey with assurance and clarity.

7

Financial Designer–Crafting Financial Stability

A goal without a plan is just a wish.

—Antoine de Saint-Exupéry

Imagine, if you will, a ship without a sail, a knight without a quest, or a burger without fries. Just as these entities seem woefully incomplete, so does your financial journey without a clearly defined goal. Let's embark on this adventure to carve out your financial dreams from the amorphous cloud of 'someday.'

Every epic quest begins with a single, albeit ambitious, goal – a beacon guiding the hero through tumultuous terrains and dragon-infested lairs. In the same vein, your financial journey requires a definitive goal, a North Star illuminating the path towards fiscal Valhalla.

SETTING FINANCIAL GOALS

Defining the Objective

Every journey needs a destination, and every book needs a

clear purpose. The main goal of this book is to help readers understand, set, and achieve their financial goals. But what does it mean to set a financial goal, and why is it so crucial?

THE ESSENCE OF FINANCIAL GOALS

Financial goals are not just numbers on a spreadsheet; they are the embodiment of our dreams, aspirations, and desires. They provide a roadmap for where we want to be and how we can get there. These goals can range from short-term objectives like saving for a vacation to long-term ambitions such as building a retirement fund.

Example 1: The Dream of Home Ownership

Consider Lisa, a young professional who dreams of buying her first home. Without a clear financial goal, this dream remains just that—a dream. By defining her objective (e.g., saving $50,000 for a down payment within five years), Lisa creates a tangible target. This goal motivates her to budget, save, and possibly invest wisely to make her dream a reality.

ENGAGING STORIES: REAL-LIFE APPLICATIONS

The Journey of John and Mary

John and Mary were newlyweds with a shared vision of financial independence. However, they quickly realized that their incomes were being frittered away on dining out and impulsive shopping. They decided to set a clear financial goal: to save $30,000 in three years for a business venture.

By defining this goal, they transformed their spending habits. They created a budget, cut down on unnecessary expenses, and started a small side hustle. Their journey was not without challenges, but their clear purpose kept them focused. Three years later, they not only reached their savings target but also developed a disciplined financial mindset that benefited them in the long run.

The Theory of Goal-Setting

Psychologist Edwin Locke's Goal-Setting Theory emphasizes the importance of clear, specific goals. According to Locke, goals serve as motivators, directing attention and effort towards activities that lead to goal attainment. Clear goals also enhance persistence and encourage the development of strategies to achieve them. This theory underscores why defining a clear purpose is fundamental to financial success.

BREAKING DOWN THE PURPOSE: ELEMENTS OF A FINANCIAL GOAL

Specificity

A goal must be specific to provide clear direction. 'Save money' is a vague intention, while 'Save $5,000 in a year' offers a concrete target. This specificity transforms a wish into an actionable plan.

MEASURABILITY

Goals should be measurable to track progress. This allows for adjustments and motivates continued effort. For example, breaking down the $5,000 annual savings goal into monthly targets of approximately $417 makes it more manageable and trackable.

ATTAINABILITY

A realistic goal takes into account current financial status and future potential. Setting an unattainable goal can lead to frustration and demotivation. It's essential to balance ambition with realism.

RELEVANCE

Goals should align with broader life aspirations and values. If financial freedom is a priority, goals like paying off debt or building an emergency fund become highly relevant. Irrelevant goals, on the other hand, may not inspire sustained effort.

TIME-BOUND

Setting a deadline creates a sense of urgency. Whether it's saving a certain amount within a year or achieving a debt-free status in five years, time-bound goals prevent procrastination and promote consistent action.

- *Consider the tale of Sir Save-A-Lot, who once believed his treasure chest would magically fill itself. Spoiler alert: it didn't. But once he set his sights on a specific goal – purchasing a modest castle by the sea – his gold started to grow.*
- *Start by visualizing your ideal financial outcome. Write it down, draw it out, make a vision board, or craft a papier-mâché sculpture if that's your thing. Then, break it down into manageable chunks – like a dragon-slaying quest divided into 'find the dragon,' 'sharpen the sword,' and 'avoid becoming dragon chow.'*

- *Studies show that individuals with clear, written goals are 42% more likely to achieve them. This is not just magic – it's science!*

STEP-BY-STEP GUIDES: BREAK DOWN COMPLEX PROCESSES INTO MANAGEABLE STEPS

Dream Big: Envision Your Financial Endgame

Introduction: The Power of Big Dreams

The first step to achieving any significant financial goal is to dream big. This means envisioning your ultimate financial endgame. It could be anything from owning a dream house, retiring early, traveling the world, or achieving financial independence. Dreaming big provides the overarching vision that fuels motivation and inspires action.

Theory: The Law of Attraction

The Law of Attraction suggests that by focusing on positive thoughts, you can bring positive experiences into your life. By envisioning your financial dreams vividly and frequently, you mentally align yourself with the actions and decisions that will help you achieve them. This psychological principle underscores the importance of dreaming big as the initial step in your financial journey.

Example: Sarah's Vision of Financial Freedom

Sarah, a marketing executive, always dreamed of retiring at 50 and traveling the world. She created a vision board filled with images of exotic destinations, financial charts, and happy moments. This daily visual reminder kept her focused and motivated, guiding her financial decisions and sacrifices along the way.

DEFINE SPECIFICS: CONVERT DREAMS INTO CONCRETE GOALS

Introduction: From Dream to Reality

Once you have a big dream, the next step is to convert that dream into specific, actionable goals. Abstract dreams need to be transformed into clear, measurable objectives to create a tangible roadmap for success.

Theory: SMART Goals Framework

The SMART framework (Specific, Measurable, Achievable, Relevant, Time-bound) is a well-established method for setting effective goals. This approach ensures that your goals are clear and reachable, providing a structured path from dream to reality.

Example: John's Retirement Plan

John dreamt of a comfortable retirement with his family. To make this a reality, he defined specific goals: saving $1 million by the age of 60. This included sub-goals such as maximizing his 401(k) contributions, investing in a diverse portfolio, and creating a detailed budget to manage expenses.

TIMELINE: SET A REALISTIC TIMEFRAME

Introduction: The Importance of Timing

Setting a timeline for your financial goals is crucial. It adds a sense of urgency and helps in planning and prioritizing your efforts. A realistic timeframe ensures that your goals are achievable and keeps you focused on the end date.

Theory: Temporal Motivation Theory

Temporal Motivation Theory posits that the perceived value of a goal increases as the deadline approaches. By setting specific deadlines, you increase your motivation to work towards achieving your financial goals within the given timeframe.

Example: Emma's Debt-Free Journey

Emma had accumulated $30,000 in student loan debt. She set a goal to pay off her debt within five years. She created a detailed timeline, outlining how much she needed to pay each month and adjusting her budget accordingly. This clear timeframe helped her stay disciplined and focused on her goal.

MILESTONES: BREAK THE GOAL INTO SMALLER, ACHIEVABLE TASKS

Introduction: The Role of Milestones

Breaking down a large goal into smaller, manageable tasks, or milestones, makes the process less overwhelming and more achievable. Milestones serve as checkpoints, allowing you to track progress and stay motivated.

Theory: The Goal-Gradient Hypothesis

The Goal-Gradient Hypothesis suggests that people tend to work harder and more efficiently as they get closer to their goal. By setting milestones, you create a series of smaller goals that maintain high levels of motivation and commitment throughout your financial journey.

Example: David's Business Expansion

David, an entrepreneur, wanted to expand his business nationally.

He broke this large goal into smaller milestones: research and development, securing funding, pilot launches in two states, and a gradual rollout to additional states. Each milestone represented a significant achievement, boosting his confidence and momentum.

REVIEW: REGULARLY ASSESS PROGRESS AND ADJUST AS NEEDED

Introduction: The Necessity of Regular Reviews

Regularly reviewing your progress ensures that you stay on track and allows for adjustments based on changing circumstances or unexpected challenges. This step involves assessing your current status, celebrating successes, and recalibrating strategies as needed.

Theory: Feedback Loop and Continuous Improvement

The concept of a feedback loop is critical in continuous improvement processes. Regular reviews provide feedback on what's working and what's not, enabling you to refine your approach and enhance your strategies for better results.

Example: Lisa's Investment Portfolio

Lisa set a goal to build a robust investment portfolio. She reviewed her investments quarterly, analyzing performance, rebalancing her assets, and adjusting her strategy based on market trends. This regular assessment helped her optimize her returns and stay aligned with her long-term financial objectives.

DETAILED STEP-BY-STEP GUIDE

1. **Dream Big: Envision Your Financial Endgame**
   - **Visualization Exercises**: Spend time visualizing your dream in detail. Imagine what your life looks like once you achieve your financial goals.
   - **Vision Boards**: Create a vision board with images and words that represent your financial dreams. Place it somewhere you can see it daily.
   - **Journaling**: Write down your financial dreams in a journal. Describe them vividly, including how you will feel when you achieve them.
2. **Define Specifics: Convert Dreams into Concrete Goals**
   - **SMART Goals Worksheet**: Use the SMART framework to outline your goals. Specify the amount you need to save, the time frame, and the steps to get there.
   - **Detailed Action Plan**: Break down your SMART goals into detailed action plans. Include specific actions, deadlines, and resources needed.
   - **Accountability Partners**: Share your goals with a trusted friend or financial advisor who can provide support and accountability.
3. **Timeline: Set a Realistic Timeframe**
   - **Milestone Calendar**: Create a calendar with key milestones and deadlines. Include regular checkpoints to assess progress.
   - **Time Management Techniques**: Use techniques like the Pomodoro Technique or time blocking to allocate time for financial planning and goal achievement.
   - **Priority Setting**: Prioritize tasks based on their impact on your overall goal. Focus on high-impact activities that move you closer to your financial endgame.

4. **Milestones: Break the Goal into Smaller, Achievable Tasks**
   o **Task Lists**: Create detailed task lists for each milestone. Include specific actions and deadlines for each task.
   o **Progress Tracking**: Use tools like spreadsheets or financial apps to track progress towards each milestone. Celebrate small wins to maintain motivation.
   o **Flexibility**: Be prepared to adjust your milestones based on new information or changing circumstances. Flexibility ensures continuous progress.
5. **Review: Regularly Assess Progress and Adjust as Needed**
   o **Monthly Reviews**: Schedule monthly reviews to assess your progress. Analyze what's working, identify challenges, and make necessary adjustments.
   o **Annual Reflections**: At the end of each year, reflect on your overall progress. Reevaluate your goals and strategies based on your experiences.
   o **Feedback Mechanisms**: Establish feedback mechanisms, such as financial advisors or accountability partners, to provide insights and recommendations.

STORIES

Henry's Financial Independence Plan

Henry, a software engineer, dreamed of achieving financial independence by the age of 45. He envisioned a life where he could work on passion projects without financial stress. Henry started by defining specific goals, such as saving $1 million and generating passive income through investments. He set a 20-year timeline and broke his goal into smaller milestones, like maxing out his 401(k) and building a diversified investment portfolio. Henry reviewed his progress quarterly, adjusting his strategy based on market performance and personal circumstances. His disciplined approach and regular assessments kept him on track, and he achieved financial independence at 44.

Theory: The Incremental Theory of Goal Setting

Incremental Theory suggests that people achieve significant goals through small, consistent steps rather than dramatic changes. This theory aligns with the step-by-step approach, emphasizing the importance of breaking down complex processes into manageable tasks. By focusing on incremental progress, individuals can maintain motivation and achieve their financial goals over time.

JESSICA'S EDUCATION FUND

Jessica wanted to save for her children's college education. She dreamed of providing them with debt-free college experiences. Jessica started by defining her goal: saving $200,000 over 18 years. She created a timeline and set milestones, such as contributing to a 529 plan monthly and increasing contributions as her income grew. Jessica reviewed her progress annually, adjusting her contributions based on changes in her financial situation. Her clear goal, timeline, and regular reviews ensured that she stayed on track, and she successfully funded her children's education.

Breaking down complex processes into manageable steps is essential for achieving financial goals. By dreaming big, defining specifics, setting realistic timelines, creating milestones, and regularly reviewing progress, you can turn abstract financial dreams into concrete realities. Through engaging stories, practical examples, and related theories, this guide provides a comprehensive approach to financial goal setting, ensuring that readers are well-equipped to navigate their financial journeys with confidence and clarity.

> *Setting goals is the first step in turning the invisible into the visible.*
>
> —Tony Robbins

THE IMPORTANCE OF VISUALIZATION

Visualization is a powerful tool in goal setting. Athletes often visualize their success before a competition, mentally rehearsing their performance. Similarly, visualizing financial goals can enhance motivation and clarity. Creating vision boards, where images and words representing financial aspirations are displayed, can keep goals in sight and top of mind.

THE ROLE OF ACCOUNTABILITY

Accountability partners or financial advisors can play a crucial role in achieving financial goals. Sharing your goals with someone who can provide support, encouragement, and constructive feedback increases the likelihood of success.

Example: The Accountability Duo

Mike and Sam, both colleagues and friends, decided to become each other's accountability partners. They shared their financial goals and met monthly to review their progress. This mutual support system kept them motivated and focused. When Mike was tempted to splurge on a new gadget, Sam reminded him of his financial goal, helping him stay on track.

THE PSYCHOLOGICAL IMPACT OF CLEAR FINANCIAL GOALS

Setting clear financial goals can also have a positive psychological impact. It reduces stress by providing a sense of control and direction. Knowing exactly what you are working towards can alleviate the anxiety that often accompanies financial uncertainty.

Example: Reduced Financial Stress

Research by the American Psychological Association shows that financial stress is a significant concern for many individuals. By setting clear financial goals, individuals can create a plan to address their financial challenges, which can reduce stress and improve overall well-being.

REAL-LIFE EXAMPLES: LEARNING FROM OTHERS

Anna's Financial Transformation

Anna was a recent college graduate with a significant amount of student loan debt. Initially overwhelmed, she decided to set a clear financial goal: pay off $20,000 of debt within two years. This goal was specific, measurable, attainable, relevant, and time-bound.

Anna's strategy included creating a strict budget, taking on a part-time job, and using any bonuses or tax refunds to pay down her debt. She tracked her progress monthly, celebrating small milestones along the way. By staying committed to her clear purpose, Anna managed to pay off her debt ahead of schedule and felt a profound sense of accomplishment.

- *Jane Doe transformed her passion for knitting into a lucrative side hustle, setting a clear goal of saving $10,000 for her dream*

vacation. She not only met her goal but exceeded it, all because she had a defined target.
- *Activity: Create a Financial Goal Worksheet. Fill in your dream, steps, timeline, and milestones. Check in with your progress every month.*

BUDGETING AND SAVING STRATEGIES

- *To turn your financial dreams into reality, you need a solid plan. Budgeting and saving are your sword and shield in this endeavor.*
- *Imagine discovering a treasure map. Exciting, right? But without the key to decipher it, you'd be as lost as a pirate without a parrot. Your budget is that key, turning vague 'X marks the spot' notions into actionable steps.*
- *Meet Bob the Budgeteer, who once thought his monthly expenses were like a mystery novel — full of unexpected twists. With a budget, he turned those plot twists into a predictable, albeit somewhat dull, accounting manual.*

PRACTICAL TIPS: IMPLEMENTING FINANCIAL GOALS

1. **Create a Financial Goals Worksheet**
   Write down your financial goals, categorize them (short-term, medium-term, long-term), and set deadlines. This worksheet serves as a constant reminder and a tracking tool.
2. **Automate Your Savings**
   Set up automatic transfers to your savings or investment accounts. This ensures consistency and removes the

temptation to spend money set aside for your goals.
3. **Review and Adjust Regularly**
   Life circumstances change, and so might your financial goals. Regularly review your progress and adjust your goals as necessary. Flexibility ensures your goals remain relevant and attainable.

- *List all your income sources. Now, list your expenses. Prioritize needs over wants. If your budget were a dinner plate, rent would be the hearty stew, while lattes are the sprinkles on a cupcake – delightful but not essential.*

   Do not save what is left after spending; instead, spend what is left after saving.

   —Warren Buffett

- *Research shows that people who budget are more likely to pay bills on time and less likely to live paycheck to paycheck. Budgeting is like brushing your teeth – not always fun, but essential for long-term health.*

STEP 1: INCOME INVENTORY: LIST ALL INCOME SOURCES

Introduction: Understanding Your Financial Foundation

The first step in any effective budgeting process is to know how much money you have coming in. This involves listing all sources of income, which provides a clear picture of your financial foundation.

Theory: Income Diversification

Income diversification is a concept where individuals earn money from multiple sources. This approach not only provides financial security but also maximizes earning potential. According to financial experts, having diverse income streams can protect you from economic downturns and job loss.

Example: John's Multiple Income Streams

John is a high school teacher who also tutors students online, writes educational content for websites, and sells handmade crafts on Etsy. By listing all his income sources, John gets a comprehensive view of his earnings, which helps him plan his budget more effectively.

STEPS TO LIST INCOME SOURCES

1. **Primary Income**: This includes your main job or business earnings.
2. **Secondary Income**: Side gigs, freelance work, and part-time jobs.
3. **Passive Income**: Investments, rental income, dividends, and royalties.
4. **Irregular Income**: Bonuses, gifts, tax refunds, and occasional earnings.

ENGAGING STORY: SARAH'S SIDE HUSTLE SUCCESS

Sarah, a graphic designer, realized that relying solely on her full-time job wasn't enough to meet her financial goals. She started offering freelance design services and selling her artwork online. Listing these additional income sources allowed Sarah to understand her true earning potential and plan her finances more strategically.

STEP 2: EXPENSE CATALOG: TRACK ALL MONTHLY EXPENSES

Introduction: The Importance of Expense Tracking

To manage your money effectively, you need to know where it's going. Tracking all monthly expenses provides insight into spending habits and identifies areas where you can save.

Theory: The Pareto Principle

The Pareto Principle, or the 80/20 rule, suggests that 80% of results come from 20% of efforts. Applied to budgeting, this means that a significant portion of your expenses might be concentrated in a few categories. Identifying these can help you make impactful changes.

Example: Emily's Expense Breakdown

Emily decided to track her expenses for a month and discovered that dining out and online shopping were her biggest spending categories. By recognizing these patterns, she was able to cut back and allocate more money towards savings.

Steps to Track Expenses

1. **Daily Tracking**: Write down every expense, no matter how small.
2. **Use Technology**: Utilize budgeting apps or spreadsheets to record expenses.
3. **Categorize Spending**: Group expenses into categories like groceries, utilities, entertainment, and transportation.
4. **Review Regularly**: Analyze your expenses weekly or monthly to stay on top of your spending.

ENGAGING STORY: MARK'S MONTHLY REVIEW

Mark, a young professional, started using a budgeting app to track his expenses. He was surprised to find out how much he spent on coffee each month. This realization helped him cut back on his daily coffee runs and instead, he started brewing his own coffee at home, saving a significant amount of money.

STEP 3: CATEGORIZE: DIVIDE EXPENSES INTO NEEDS (FIXED) AND WANTS (VARIABLE)

Introduction: Differentiating Between Needs and Wants

Not all expenses are created equal. Dividing your expenses into needs (fixed) and wants (variable) helps prioritize spending and identify areas for potential savings.

Theory: Maslow's Hierarchy of Needs

Maslow's Hierarchy of Needs can be applied to budgeting by distinguishing between essential and non-essential expenses. Basic needs like food, shelter, and utilities are critical for survival, while wants are additional comforts that enhance quality of life.

Example: Fixed vs. Variable Expenses

- **Fixed Expenses**: Rent/mortgage, utilities, insurance, loan payments.
- **Variable Expenses**: Dining out, entertainment, vacations, shopping.

STEPS TO CATEGORIZE EXPENSES

1. **Identify Fixed Needs**: List non-negotiable expenses necessary for daily living.

2. **Identify Variable Wants**: List discretionary expenses that can be adjusted or eliminated.
3. **Prioritize**: Focus on covering fixed needs first, then allocate the remaining funds to wants.
4. **Adjust as Needed**: Regularly review and re-categorize expenses based on changing priorities.

ENGAGING STORY: RACHEL'S REALIZATION

Rachel, a college student, categorized her expenses and realized that her monthly streaming subscriptions were adding up to a significant amount. By cutting down on unnecessary subscriptions, she was able to save more money for textbooks and other essentials.

STEP 4: ALLOCATE FUNDS: PRIORITIZE NEEDS, THEN ALLOCATE FUNDS FOR WANTS

Introduction: Creating a Balanced Budget

Once you've categorized your expenses, the next step is to allocate funds accordingly. Prioritizing needs ensures that essential expenses are covered before addressing wants.

Theory: Zero-Based Budgeting

Zero-Based Budgeting is a method where every dollar is assigned a job, ensuring that income minus expenses equals zero. This method helps prioritize spending and ensures that money is allocated efficiently.

Example: Amanda's Budget Allocation

Amanda's monthly income is $3,000. She allocates $1,200

for rent, $300 for utilities, $400 for groceries, and $200 for transportation (fixed needs). The remaining $900 is divided between savings, dining out, entertainment, and personal shopping (variable wants).

STEPS TO ALLOCATE FUNDS

1. **List Fixed Expenses**: Deduct these from your total income first.
2. **List Variable Expenses**: Allocate remaining funds to these categories.
3. **Savings and Investments**: Prioritize saving a portion of your income.
4. **Flexibility**: Be prepared to adjust allocations based on actual spending and changing priorities.

ENGAGING STORY: DAVID'S BUDGETING JOURNEY

David, an IT consultant, struggled with overspending on luxury items. By adopting zero-based budgeting, he allocated specific amounts to each category and stuck to his budget. This disciplined approach helped him save more and reduce unnecessary expenses.

STEP 5: ADJUST AND MONITOR: REGULARLY REVIEW AND TWEAK YOUR BUDGET

Introduction: The Dynamic Nature of Budgeting

A budget is not a set-it-and-forget-it tool. Regularly reviewing and adjusting your budget is crucial to stay on track and accommodate changes in income or expenses.

Theory: The Agile Budgeting Approach

Agile budgeting is a flexible approach that allows for regular adjustments based on real-time financial data. This method encourages frequent reviews and adaptations to align with current financial conditions.

Example: Laura's Monthly Budget Reviews

Laura, a freelance writer, has an irregular income. She reviews her budget monthly to adjust for fluctuations in her earnings. This proactive approach helps her manage her finances effectively, even with variable income.

STEPS TO ADJUST AND MONITOR BUDGET

1. **Monthly Reviews**: Set a date each month to review your budget.
2. **Analyze Variances**: Compare actual spending to your budgeted amounts.
3. **Identify Trends**: Look for patterns in your spending habits.
4. **Adjust Accordingly**: Reallocate funds based on your findings.
5. **Set New Goals**: Update your financial goals as needed.

ENGAGING STORY: MICHAEL'S BUDGET EVOLUTION

Michael, a sales manager, found that his budget often didn't match his actual spending. By conducting monthly reviews, he identified areas where he was consistently overspending and adjusted his budget accordingly. This continuous improvement process helped him stay on track and achieve his financial goals.

Breaking down complex financial processes into manageable

steps is essential for effective budgeting and financial management. By following a structured guide that includes income inventory, expense tracking, categorization, fund allocation, and regular adjustments, you can achieve financial stability and reach your goals. Through engaging stories, practical examples, and related theories, this guide provides a comprehensive approach to managing your finances with confidence and clarity.

Beware of little expenses; a small leak will sink a great ship.

—Benjamin Franklin

- *Sarah meticulously tracked her spending, cutting out unnecessary costs like her subscription to the Monthly Cheese Club. She saved enough to start an emergency fund and felt like she conquered her own little financial Everest.*
- *Activity: Create a detailed monthly budget. Track your expenses for a month and compare them against your budget. Adjust as necessary.*

INVESTING IN YOUR FUTURE

- *Let's take your financial savvy to the next level – making your money work for you like a legion of diligent dwarves in a fantasy mine.*
- *If budgeting is the bread and butter of financial health, investing is the gourmet cheese platter. It's time to make your money sprout wings and soar.*
- *Remember Mildred the Money Maven, who thought investing was only for the ultra-wealthy? She started small with her spare change, and now her portfolio looks like a treasure chest.*
- *Start with understanding the basics: stocks, bonds, mutual funds. Think of these as different classes of magical items,*

each with its unique properties and potential. Diversify your investments to spread risk – like not putting all your enchanted eggs in one dragon's nest.
- *Studies indicate that those who start investing early can harness the power of compound interest – your money earning money. It's like planting a magic bean that grows into a beanstalk laden with golden coins.*

INTRODUCTION: THE IMPORTANCE OF STEP-BY-STEP INVESTMENT GUIDES

Investing can often seem overwhelming, especially for beginners. The key to overcoming this complexity is to break the process down into manageable steps. By doing so, you can approach investing systematically, making informed decisions that align with your financial goals and risk tolerance. Let's explore a detailed step-by-step guide to successful investing.

STEP 1: EDUCATION: LEARN THE BASICS OF DIFFERENT INVESTMENT TYPES

Introduction: Building a Strong Foundation

The first step in investing is to educate yourself about the different types of investments available. Understanding the basics will empower you to make informed decisions and build a diversified portfolio.

Theory: Financial Literacy and Investment Knowledge

Financial literacy is the ability to understand and effectively use various financial skills, including personal financial management, budgeting, and investing. A solid foundation in financial literacy is essential for making informed investment decisions. Studies have shown that individuals with higher financial literacy are more likely to participate in the stock market and other investment opportunities.

TYPES OF INVESTMENTS

1. **Stocks**: Represent ownership in a company and entitle you to a portion of its profits. Stocks are known for their high potential returns but also come with higher risk.
2. **Bonds**: Debt securities issued by corporations or governments. They provide regular interest payments and are considered lower risk compared to stocks.
3. **Mutual Funds**: Pooled funds from multiple investors, managed by a professional. They offer diversification and are less risky than individual stocks.
4. **ETFs (Exchange-Traded Funds)**: Similar to mutual funds but trade like stocks. They provide diversification and liquidity.
5. **Real Estate**: Investment in property. It can generate rental income and appreciate in value over time.
6. **Commodities**: Physical goods like gold, silver, oil, and agricultural products. They are often used as a hedge against inflation.

Example: Maria's Investment Learning Journey

Maria, a 30-year-old marketing executive, wanted to start investing but felt overwhelmed by the jargon and complexity. She took an online course on investment basics, read books like 'The Intelligent Investor' by Benjamin Graham, and followed financial news. This education gave her the confidence to start investing and make informed decisions.

STEP 2: ASSESS RISK TOLERANCE: UNDERSTAND HOW MUCH RISK YOU CAN COMFORTABLY HANDLE

Introduction: Balancing Risk and Reward

Assessing your risk tolerance is crucial before making any investments. It determines how much risk you can handle without losing sleep over market fluctuations.

Theory: Risk Tolerance and Investor Behavior

Risk tolerance refers to an investor's ability to endure market volatility and potential loss of investment capital. Factors influencing risk tolerance include age, income, financial goals, and investment experience. Understanding your risk tolerance helps in choosing the right investments and avoiding panic during market downturns.

STEPS TO ASSESS RISK TOLERANCE

1. **Evaluate Financial Situation**: Consider your income, expenses, savings, and debt.
2. **Set Financial Goals**: Short-term and long-term goals influence risk tolerance.
3. **Questionnaires and Tools**: Use risk assessment questionnaires available online.
4. **Past Behavior**: Reflect on how you've reacted to financial losses in the past.

Example: John's Risk Assessment

John, a 45-year-old engineer, took a risk tolerance questionnaire and discovered he was a conservative investor. He preferred investments that offered stability and regular income, such as bonds and dividend-paying stocks, over high-risk growth stocks.

STEP 3: START SMALL: BEGIN WITH A MANAGEABLE AMOUNT

Introduction: The Importance of Starting Small

Starting small allows you to learn and gain experience without risking significant capital. It also helps build confidence as you become more familiar with the investment process.

Theory: Dollar-Cost Averaging

Dollar-cost averaging is an investment strategy where you invest a fixed amount of money at regular intervals, regardless of the market conditions. This approach reduces the impact of volatility and lowers the average cost per share over time.

Example: Emily's First Investment

Emily, a recent college graduate, started her investment journey by setting aside $100 per month into a diversified ETF. This manageable amount allowed her to get comfortable with investing and understand how the market works without risking too much of her savings.

STEPS TO START SMALL

1. **Set Aside a Fixed Amount**: Decide on a small, manageable amount to invest regularly.
2. **Choose Low-Cost Investments**: Look for investments with low fees, such as index funds or ETFs.
3. **Automate Investments**: Set up automatic transfers to your investment account.

4. **Monitor Progress**: Track your investments and learn from the outcomes.

STEP 4: DIVERSIFY: SPREAD YOUR INVESTMENTS ACROSS VARIOUS ASSETS

Introduction: The Power of Diversification

Diversification is a risk management strategy that involves spreading your investments across different asset classes to reduce risk.

Theory: Modern Portfolio Theory

Modern Portfolio Theory (MPT), developed by Harry Markowitz, suggests that diversification can optimize a portfolio's return by reducing its risk. According to MPT, a diversified portfolio is less volatile because the performance of different assets is not perfectly correlated.

STEPS TO DIVERSIFY YOUR PORTFOLIO

1. **Asset Allocation**: Decide on the percentage of your portfolio to allocate to stocks, bonds, real estate, and other assets.
2. **Geographic Diversification**: Invest in both domestic and international markets.
3. **Sector Diversification**: Spread investments across various sectors such as technology, healthcare, and consumer goods.
4. **Rebalance Regularly**: Adjust your portfolio periodically to maintain your desired asset allocation.

Example: David's Diversified Portfolio

David, a 35-year-old software developer, created a diversified portfolio by investing in U.S. stocks, international stocks, bonds, and real estate. He allocated 50% to stocks (30% U.S. and 20% international), 30% to bonds, and 20% to real estate. This diversification helped him achieve a balance between growth and stability.

STEP 5: MONITOR AND ADJUST: REGULARLY REVIEW AND ADJUST YOUR PORTFOLIO

Introduction: The Necessity of Ongoing Management

Investing is not a one-time activity. Regularly monitoring and adjusting your portfolio ensures that it remains aligned with your financial goals and risk tolerance.

Theory: The Feedback Loop

A feedback loop involves using the results of your actions to adjust your behavior. In investing, regularly reviewing your portfolio's performance and making necessary adjustments based on market conditions and personal goals create a positive feedback loop that enhances investment success.

STEPS TO MONITOR AND ADJUST YOUR PORTFOLIO

1. **Set Review Intervals**: Review your portfolio monthly, quarterly, or annually.
2. **Analyze Performance**: Compare the performance of your investments against benchmarks.
3. **Rebalance**: Adjust your portfolio to maintain your desired asset allocation.
4. **Stay Informed**: Keep up with market news and trends to make informed decisions.

Example: Laura's Portfolio Management

Laura, a financial analyst, set up quarterly reviews for her investment portfolio. She analyzed the performance of each asset, rebalanced her portfolio to maintain her desired allocation, and adjusted her strategy based on market conditions. This proactive approach helped her maximize returns and manage risk effectively.

ENGAGING STORIES AND THEORIES

MICHAEL'S INVESTMENT EDUCATION JOURNEY

Michael, a high school teacher, felt intimidated by the stock market. He started by attending local investment workshops and reading books on personal finance. This education helped him understand different investment types and their risks, giving him the confidence to start investing in index funds and blue-chip stocks.

SARAH'S RISK ASSESSMENT REVELATION

Sarah, a 28-year-old nurse, initially thought she could handle high-risk investments. However, after a market downturn left her anxious, she reassessed her risk tolerance and shifted her portfolio towards more stable investments like bonds and dividend-paying stocks. This change helped her feel more secure and aligned her investments with her true risk tolerance.

EMMA'S DOLLAR-COST AVERAGING SUCCESS

Emma, a graphic designer, adopted a dollar-cost averaging

strategy, investing $200 monthly into a diversified mutual fund. This approach allowed her to take advantage of market fluctuations and steadily build her investment portfolio without trying to time the market.

DAVID'S DIVERSIFICATION STRATEGY

David, an entrepreneur, diversified his investments by spreading them across different asset classes and geographic regions. He invested in U.S. stocks, emerging market funds, real estate, and commodities. This diversification protected his portfolio from significant losses during market downturns and ensured steady growth over time.

ALEX'S PORTFOLIO ADJUSTMENT ROUTINE

Alex, a business consultant, made it a habit to review his investment portfolio every six months. He used a spreadsheet to track performance, analyzed market trends, and rebalanced his portfolio to maintain his desired asset allocation. This disciplined approach helped him stay on track with his financial goals and adapt to changing market conditions.

Breaking down the complex process of investing into manageable steps makes it accessible and achievable for everyone. By educating yourself, assessing your risk tolerance, starting small, diversifying your investments, and regularly monitoring and adjusting your portfolio, you can build a successful investment strategy. Through engaging stories, practical examples, and related theories, this guide provides a comprehensive approach to investing, ensuring that you are well-equipped to navigate the financial markets with confidence and clarity.

> *The stock market is filled with individuals who know the price of everything, but the value of nothing.*
>
> —Philip Fisher

- *John began investing in index funds with just $50 a month. Ten years later, he has a portfolio that's robust enough to withstand financial storms.*
- *Activity: Research and list different types of investments. Create a hypothetical portfolio and track its progress over six months.*

Defining the main goal of the book – setting financial goals – is akin to laying the foundation of a sturdy house. It provides structure, direction, and purpose. Through relatable stories, practical tips, and psychological insights, this book aims to transform the abstract concept of financial goals into a tangible, achievable reality. By following the principles outlined, readers can embark on a journey towards financial stability and success, equipped with the knowledge and motivation to turn their dreams into attainable goals.

8

Health Innovator–Creating a Balanced Lifestyle

CLEAR PURPOSE:

The aim of this chapter is to guide readers in achieving a balanced lifestyle through practical health, fitness, and mental wellness strategies. We will explore the pillars of a balanced lifestyle, diving deep into nutrition, fitness fundamentals, mental health practices, and the art of balancing work, play, and rest. This comprehensive approach ensures readers are well-equipped to make lasting changes that promote overall well-being and fulfillment.

ENGAGING INTRODUCTION:

Welcome, dear reader, to the quest of becoming a Health Innovator! Imagine your body as a highly tuned sports car; to keep it running smoothly, you need premium fuel, regular maintenance, and some top-notch polishing. Ready to turbocharge your life? Think of this chapter as your pit crew, here to provide you with the tools and strategies to keep you performing at your best. From the foods you eat to the way you move and rest, every aspect plays a crucial role in your journey toward a balanced lifestyle. Let's embark on this exciting adventure together!

THE NUTRITION SPECTRUM: FUELING YOUR BODY

1. **Understanding Macronutrients:**
   - **Proteins, Carbohydrates, and Fats:** Learn about the role of each macronutrient in the body. Proteins are essential for muscle repair and growth, carbohydrates provide energy, and fats support cell function and hormone production.
   - **Balanced Plate:** Visualize your plate divided into sections: half for fruits and vegetables, a quarter for lean proteins, and a quarter for whole grains. This ensures a balanced intake of essential nutrients.
2. **Micronutrients Matter:**
   - **Vitamins and Minerals:** Dive into the importance of micronutrients such as vitamins A, C, D, and minerals like iron, calcium, and magnesium. Understand their roles in maintaining health, from boosting immunity to supporting bone health.
   - **Superfoods:** Highlight nutrient-dense foods like kale, blueberries, and quinoa that pack a powerful punch of vitamins and minerals in every bite.
3. **Hydration: The Forgotten Hero:**
   - **Importance of Water:** Discover the critical role water plays in bodily functions, including temperature regulation, joint lubrication, and waste removal.
   - **Hydration Tips:** Incorporate practical tips like carrying a reusable water bottle, setting hydration reminders, and consuming water-rich foods like cucumbers and watermelons.

FITNESS FUNDAMENTALS: MOVING FOR HEALTH

1. **Finding Your Fitness Passion:**
   - **Explore Different Activities:** From traditional gym workouts to unconventional activities like rock climbing, dancing, or martial arts, find what excites you and keeps you moving.
   - **Case Study:** Jane discovered her love for Zumba during a friend's class, transforming her fitness routine from a chore to a joy.
2. **Creating a Balanced Workout Routine:**
   - **Strength, Cardio, and Flexibility:** Balance your routine with strength training for muscle health, cardio for heart health, and flexibility exercises for joint mobility.
   - **Weekly Plan Example:** A sample week might include three days of strength training, two days of cardio, and daily stretching or yoga sessions.
3. **Overcoming Exercise Barriers:**
   - **Time Management:** Fit exercise into your busy schedule by breaking workouts into shorter sessions or incorporating movement into daily activities.
   - **Motivation Strategies:** Use techniques like setting SMART goals, tracking progress, and finding a workout buddy for accountability.

MENTAL HEALTH AND SELF-CARE PRACTICES

1. **The Power of Mindfulness:**
   - **Mindfulness Meditation:** Learn simple techniques to practice mindfulness, such as focusing on your breath, doing a body scan, or engaging in mindful eating.
   - **Story:** Mark used mindfulness to manage work-related

stress, finding peace and clarity even during hectic days.
2. **Building Resilience:**
   - **Positive Psychology:** Understand the principles of positive psychology, including gratitude, optimism, and building on strengths.
   - **Exercise:** Start a gratitude journal to note three things you're thankful for each day, fostering a positive outlook.
3. **Creating a Self-Care Routine:**
   - **Daily Practices:** Incorporate daily self-care activities like reading, taking walks, or enjoying a hobby.
   - **Example:** Sarah starts her day with a 10-minute meditation and ends it with a relaxing bath, creating bookends of calm in her day.

BALANCING WORK, PLAY, AND REST

1. **Work-Life Harmony:**
   - **Setting Boundaries:** Learn to set healthy boundaries between work and personal life, such as turning off work emails after hours.
   - **Flexible Schedules:** Explore the benefits of flexible work arrangements, like telecommuting or flexible hours, to better balance responsibilities.
2. **The Art of Play:**
   - **Importance of Leisure:** Understand the psychological benefits of play, including stress relief and increased creativity.
   - **Ideas for Play:** Engage in activities like board games, sports, or creative arts to bring joy and relaxation into your life.
3. **Prioritizing Rest:**
   - **Sleep Hygiene:** Adopt practices for better sleep, such

as maintaining a consistent sleep schedule, creating a restful environment, and avoiding screens before bed.
- **Restorative Practices:** Incorporate relaxation techniques like progressive muscle relaxation, deep breathing exercises, and nature walks.

REAL-LIFE STORIES: TRANSFORMATIONS AND TRIUMPHS

1. **Bob's Journey to Health:**
   - **Background:** Bob was an overworked accountant whose poor lifestyle choices led to a health scare.
   - **Transformation:** By adopting balanced nutrition, regular exercise, and mindfulness practices, Bob transformed his health and regained vitality.
2. **Jane's Fitness Revelation:**
   - **Background:** Jane struggled with finding joy in fitness until she discovered Zumba.
   - **Transformation:** Embracing Zumba not only improved her physical health but also boosted her mood and social connections.
3. **Mark's Mindfulness Success:**
   - **Background:** Mark faced intense work stress that affected his mental health.
   - **Transformation:** Through mindfulness meditation, Mark found peace, clarity, and improved productivity.

THEORIES AND RESEARCH: BACKING IT UP WITH SCIENCE

1. **Nutrition Science:**
   - **Studies on Balanced Diets:** Research shows that a

balanced diet rich in fruits, vegetables, and whole grains can prevent chronic diseases.
- **Case Example:** The Mediterranean diet, known for its balanced approach, has been linked to lower rates of heart disease and longer life expectancy.

2. **Exercise Physiology:**
   - **Benefits of Regular Exercise:** Scientific evidence supports the benefits of regular physical activity, including reduced risk of chronic diseases, improved mental health, and longer life.
   - **Case Example:** A study from the American Heart Association shows that just 150 minutes of moderate exercise per week can significantly improve cardiovascular health.

3. **Psychological Well-being:**
   - **Mindfulness and Mental Health:** Research indicates that mindfulness practices can reduce symptoms of anxiety and depression, improve focus, and enhance overall well being.
   - **Case Example:** A Harvard study found that mindfulness meditation can actually change brain structures, enhancing areas related to self-awareness and compassion.

PRACTICAL TIPS AND STEP-BY-STEP GUIDES

1. **Nutrition Overhaul:**
   - **Week 1:** Track your current eating habits and identify areas for improvement.
   - **Week 2:** Gradually replace unhealthy snacks with nutritious options.
   - **Week 3:** Plan balanced meals and try new healthy recipes.

- **Week 4:** Continue building on healthy habits and reflect on progress.
2. **Fitness Routine:**
   - **Month 1:** Start with 20-minute daily walks and light stretching.
   - **Month 2:** Incorporate strength training exercises twice a week.
   - **Month 3:** Add variety with new activities like swimming or cycling.
   - **Month 4:** Set specific fitness goals and track your achievements.
3. **Mindfulness Practice:**
   - **Week 1:** Begin with 5-minute daily meditation sessions.
   - **Week 2:** Increase meditation time to 10 minutes and explore different techniques.
   - **Week 3:** Incorporate mindfulness into daily activities, like eating and walking.
   - **Week 4:** Reflect on changes in your stress levels and overall well-being.

INSPIRATIONAL QUOTES

Health is a state of complete harmony of the body, mind, and spirit.

—B.K.S. Iyengar

To keep the body in good health is a duty… otherwise, we shall not be able to keep our mind strong and clear.

—Buddha

REAL-LIFE EXAMPLES AND SUCCESS STORIES

1. **Sarah's Self-Care Transformation:**
   - **Background:** Sarah juggled a demanding job and family responsibilities, often neglecting her own needs.
   - **Transformation:** By integrating self-care practices like meditation and mindful eating, Sarah found balance and improved her overall well-being.
2. **Mike's Fitness Journey:**
   - **Background:** Mike struggled with weight and health issues due to a sedentary lifestyle.
   - **Transformation:** Committing to a fitness routine and balanced diet, Mike lost weight, gained strength, and discovered a new passion for running.
3. **Emily's Mental Health Triumph:**
   - **Background:** Emily battled anxiety and depression for years, impacting her quality of life.
   - **Transformation:** Through therapy, mindfulness, and support groups, Emily learned to manage her mental health and now helps others as a peer counselor.

EXERCISES AND ACTIVITIES

1. **Nutrition Challenge:**
   - **Track Your Intake:** Keep a food diary for a week and identify patterns.
   - **Healthy Swaps:** Replace one unhealthy food item with a healthier option each day.
   - **Cook at Home:** Try cooking a new healthy recipe each week.
2. **Fitness Challenge:**
   - **Daily Movement:** Commit to at least 30 minutes of physical activity every day.

- **Try Something New:** Experiment with different types of exercise to find what you enjoy most.
- **Progress Tracking:** Keep a log of your workouts and celebrate milestones.
3. **Mindfulness Challenge:**
   - **Daily Meditation:** Start with 5-10 minutes of meditation each morning.
   - **Mindful Moments:** Practice mindfulness during everyday activities like eating and walking.
   - **Reflection Journal:** Write about your mindfulness experiences and how they affect your mood and stress levels.

SUMMARY AND NEXT STEPS

As we wrap up this extensive journey towards becoming a Health Innovator, remember that the key to a balanced lifestyle lies in integrating practical health, fitness, and mental wellness strategies into your daily routine. By taking small, consistent steps and making gradual changes, you can achieve lasting well-being and fulfillment. Reflect on your progress, set new goals, and continue to explore ways to enhance your health and happiness. Your journey doesn't end here – it's just the beginning of a vibrant and balanced life.

So, dear reader, strap in and get ready to turbocharge your life. Embrace the journey of becoming a Health Innovator, and watch as you transform into the best version of yourself. Here's to a healthier, happier, and more balanced you!

RELATABLE STORIES:

Larkin's Journey:

Meet Larkin, an overworked accountant who thought 'wellness' was something only yogis and health nuts cared about. His diet consisted of coffee and vending machine snacks, and exercise meant lifting his TV remote. One day, Larkin's body decided enough was enough, and he ended up in the hospital with severe exhaustion. That was Larkin's wake-up call. Today, Larkin is a health enthusiast, balancing his work with nutritious meals, regular workouts, and meditation sessions. His transformation wasn't instant, but step by step, he became the health innovator of his own life.

EMMA'S AWAKENING:

Emma was a high-powered executive working in a competitive corporate environment. Her days were filled with meetings, deadlines, and working lunches consisting of fast food and sugary snacks. Emma prided herself on her work ethic but paid little attention to her health. Her turning point came when she fainted during a crucial board meeting due to extreme stress and poor nutrition. Shaken by the incident, Emma decided to take control of her health.

She began by consulting a nutritionist who helped her understand the importance of balanced meals. Slowly, Emma replaced her fast-food lunches with salads, lean proteins, and whole grains. She incorporated yoga into her daily routine to manage stress and improve flexibility. Over time, Emma noticed a significant improvement in her energy levels and mental clarity. Her productivity soared, and she became a role model for her colleagues, proving that even the busiest professionals can prioritize health.

RAJ'S REALIZATION:

Raj, a software engineer, spent most of his time in front of a computer screen. Late-night coding sessions fueled by energy drinks and junk food were the norm. Physical activity was nonexistent, and Raj's weight steadily increased. His wake-up call came when his doctor diagnosed him with prediabetes and warned him of the serious health risks.

Determined to make a change, Raj joined a local gym and started with basic cardio exercises. He found a community of supportive individuals who encouraged him to keep going. Raj also attended nutrition workshops and learned how to cook healthy meals. He replaced his energy drinks with green tea and smoothies, and his junk food with fresh fruits and nuts. As he lost weight and improved his fitness, Raj's confidence grew. He even participated in a charity run, something he never imagined he could do. Raj's journey from a sedentary lifestyle to an active one inspired many of his friends and family to embark on their health journeys.

MIA'S TRANSFORMATION:

Mia, a single mother of two, struggled to balance work, childcare, and self-care. Her meals were often whatever she could grab on the go, and she rarely had time for exercise. Mia's turning point came when she couldn't keep up with her children at the park and felt out of breath after just a few minutes of playing.

Determined to be a healthy role model for her kids, Mia started small. She began by preparing simple, healthy meals that she and her children could enjoy together. She involved them in cooking, turning it into a fun family activity. Mia also started taking short walks in the evening with her kids, gradually increasing the distance as her fitness improved.

Mia introduced 'family fitness time,' where they played active games, went biking, or did yoga together. This not only improved her health but also strengthened their bond. Mia's persistence paid off as she lost weight, gained energy, and felt more confident in her ability to care for her family. Her story is a testament to the power of small, consistent changes and the impact of a supportive family environment.

CARLOS' COMEBACK:

Carlos, a former athlete, had let his fitness slide after entering a demanding sales job. Long hours on the road, client dinners, and a lack of routine led to weight gain and decreased stamina. The final straw was a picture of himself at a family gathering where he barely recognized the person in the photo.

Carlos decided it was time to reclaim his health. He started by reintroducing morning runs, a habit he enjoyed during his athletic days. Carlos also joined a local sports club, rekindling his passion for competition and camaraderie. He swapped heavy client dinners for healthier options and made a point to stay active even while traveling, using hotel gyms or exploring new cities on foot.

Carlos' journey wasn't easy, but his athletic background helped him stay disciplined. He set specific goals, tracked his progress, and celebrated his achievements. Over time, Carlos not only regained his physical fitness but also found that his renewed energy and confidence positively impacted his professional life. His story shows that it's never too late to get back on track and that past habits can be powerful allies in new endeavors.

SOPHIA'S SELF-CARE REVOLUTION:

Sophia, a nurse, spent her days caring for others but neglected her own health. Long shifts, irregular meals, and insufficient sleep took a toll on her well-being. Her wake-up call came when she experienced burnout and realized she couldn't pour from an empty cup.

Determined to practice what she preached, Sophia committed to a self-care routine. She started with proper hydration, carrying a water bottle to ensure she stayed hydrated throughout her shifts. Sophia also prioritized sleep, creating a bedtime routine to improve her sleep quality. She introduced meal prepping on her days off, ensuring she had nutritious meals ready for her hectic schedule.

Sophia also discovered the benefits of mindfulness and meditation. She used short breaks to practice deep breathing exercises, reducing her stress levels and improving her focus. Over time, Sophia found that her health and job performance improved significantly. Her journey highlights the importance of self-care for caregivers and the impact of small, sustainable changes.

MARK'S MENTAL WELLNESS JOURNEY:

Mark, a high-stress lawyer, constantly battled anxiety and insomnia. His job demanded long hours and intense focus, leaving little time for relaxation. Mark's turning point was a panic attack that struck during a crucial trial, leading him to seek help.

Mark began seeing a therapist who introduced him to

cognitive-behavioral techniques to manage stress and anxiety. He also started practicing mindfulness meditation, dedicating a few minutes each day to clear his mind. Mark found solace in physical activity, joining a local boxing gym where he could release tension.

Gradually, Mark incorporated more healthy habits into his routine. He set boundaries to ensure work didn't consume his personal life, such as turning off his phone after hours and dedicating weekends to family and hobbies. These changes transformed Mark's life, reducing his anxiety and improving his sleep. His story underscores the importance of mental health and the power of professional support combined with personal effort.

LEAH'S LIFELONG LEARNING:

Leah, a retired teacher, felt lost and lethargic after leaving the structured environment of her job. Her days lacked purpose, and her physical health began to decline. Leah's turning point was a community health fair where she learned about the benefits of lifelong learning and active aging.

Inspired, Leah enrolled in a local community college, taking courses in nutrition and fitness. She joined a senior walking club and started participating in group exercise classes. Leah also embraced technology, using fitness apps to track her activity and meal planning.

Leah's new routine brought structure and purpose to her days. She made new friends, learned new skills, and regained her physical vitality. Leah's story illustrates that it's never too late to start anew and that continuous learning and community involvement can profoundly impact health and well-being.

THEO'S TECHNOLOGICAL TRANSFORMATION:

Theo, a tech-savvy entrepreneur, spent most of his day seated at a desk, coding and managing his startup. His sedentary lifestyle led to back pain and poor posture. Theo's wake-up call was a severe back spasm that left him bedridden for days.

Determined to make a change, Theo used his love for technology to improve his health. He invested in a standing desk and ergonomic chair to support better posture. Theo also used fitness apps to schedule regular breaks for stretching and walking. He started following online fitness tutorials and joined virtual yoga classes to improve flexibility and strength.

Theo also tracked his nutrition using a meal planning app, ensuring he ate balanced meals despite his busy schedule. His tech-driven approach to health allowed Theo to seamlessly integrate wellness into his life, reducing his back pain and improving his overall fitness. Theo's journey highlights the power of technology in supporting health and the importance of ergonomics in a digital age.

THEORIES AND RESEARCH SUPPORTING HEALTH TRANSFORMATION

Behavioral Change Theory:

Behavioral change theories, such as the Transtheoretical Model (Stages of Change), emphasize that change is a process that occurs in stages: precontemplation, contemplation, preparation, action, and maintenance. Understanding this model can help individuals recognize their stage and take appropriate steps toward health improvements.

SOCIAL COGNITIVE THEORY:

Developed by Albert Bandura, this theory suggests that observing others' behaviors, attitudes, and outcomes can influence an individual's own actions. Stories like those of Larkin, Emma, Raj, and others provide powerful examples that can motivate readers to initiate their health transformations.

SELF-DETERMINATION THEORY:

This theory emphasizes both intrinsic and extrinsic motivations as key drivers of behavior. It posits that individuals are more likely to maintain healthy habits when they experience autonomy, competence, and social connection. By setting personal health objectives, acquiring new skills, and engaging with supportive communities, people can achieve greater satisfaction and enduring success.

POSITIVE PSYCHOLOGY:

Positive psychology emphasizes strengths, virtues, and factors that contribute to a fulfilling life. Incorporating elements such as gratitude, optimism, and resilience into health journeys can enhance overall well-being and provide motivation for sustained change.

MINDFULNESS AND STRESS REDUCTION:

Research has shown that mindfulness practices, such as meditation and deep breathing, can reduce stress, improve mental health, and enhance overall quality of life. Techniques like these were integral to the journeys of Mark, Sophia, and others who faced high-stress environments.

NUTRITIONAL SCIENCE:

Studies indicate that balanced nutrition is crucial for maintaining health and preventing chronic diseases. Diets rich in fruits, vegetables, whole grains, and lean proteins support physical and mental well-being, as demonstrated in the transformations of Emma, Raj, and Leah.

EXERCISE PHYSIOLOGY:

Regular physical activity is linked to numerous health benefits, including improved cardiovascular health, increased muscle strength, and enhanced mental health. The fitness journeys of Carlos, Mia, and Theo highlight the transformative power of incorporating exercise into daily routines.

These relatable stories and supporting theories provide a comprehensive look at how individuals from various backgrounds and circumstances can achieve remarkable health transformations. Each journey underscores the importance of small, consistent changes, the power of community and support, and the impact of integrating health into all aspects of life. By drawing inspiration from these examples and understanding the underlying principles, readers can embark on their own paths to becoming health innovators.

PRACTICAL TIPS:

1. **Nutrition and Fitness Fundamentals:**
   - **Eat the Rainbow:** Aim for a colorful plate with a variety of fruits and vegetables. Each color provides different essential nutrients.
   - **Hydration Station:** Drink water like it's going out of

fashion. Your body is 60% water, so keep it topped up!
- **Move It:** You don't need to be a gym rat. Find an activity you love, be it dancing, hiking, or even gardening. Consistency is key.

2. **Mental Health and Self-Care Practices:**
   - **Mindfulness Magic:** Spend 10 minutes each day in mindfulness meditation. Focus on your breath, and let the worries float away.
   - **Sleep Sanctuary:** Create a restful environment. Ditch the screens an hour before bed and let your bedroom be a sleep-only zone.

3. **Balancing Work, Play, and Rest:**
   - **Work Smart:** Use techniques like the Pomodoro Technique to stay productive without burnout.
   - **Play Hard:** Schedule fun activities weekly. Whether it's a hobby, a sport, or just a chill evening with friends, make time for joy.
   - **Rest Well:** Ensure you get 7-9 hours of sleep. Remember, even machines need downtime to function properly.

RESEARCH-BASED INSIGHTS:

Mental Health and Exercise:

1. **Anxiety and Depression Reduction:**
   - **American Psychological Association Findings:** Regular physical activity has been proven to significantly reduce symptoms of anxiety and depression. This is due to the release of endorphins, which are natural mood lifters. Additionally, exercise can distract from daily worries, provide social interaction, and improve self-esteem.
   - **Case Study:** Emily, who struggled with anxiety, found

that joining a local running club not only improved her physical health but also her mental well-being. The sense of community and the regular endorphin boosts from running helped her manage her anxiety more effectively.
2. **Cognitive Benefits:**
   - **Neuroplasticity and Exercise:** Studies indicate that physical activity promotes neuroplasticity, which is the brain's ability to adapt and reorganize itself. This can enhance cognitive functions like memory and learning.
   - **Example:** Seniors participating in regular aerobic exercise programs show improved memory and cognitive function, reducing the risk of dementia and Alzheimer's disease.

NUTRITION AND CHRONIC DISEASE PREVENTION:

1. **Balanced Diet and Chronic Diseases:**
   - **Harvard Studies:** Research from Harvard University indicates that a balanced diet rich in fruits, vegetables, whole grains, and lean proteins can prevent chronic diseases such as heart disease, diabetes, and certain cancers. These foods provide essential nutrients that support bodily functions and reduce inflammation.
   - **Case Example:** John's family has a history of heart disease. By adopting a Mediterranean diet rich in healthy fats, fruits, and vegetables, John not only improved his heart health but also experienced increased energy levels and better overall health.
2. **Impact on Immunity:**
   - **Nutrient-Rich Diets:** Consuming a diet high in vitamins and minerals strengthens the immune system, making it easier to fend off infections. Nutrients like

vitamin C, vitamin D, and zinc play crucial roles in maintaining a robust immune response.
- **Example:** During flu season, families who prioritize a balanced diet with plenty of fruits, vegetables, and lean proteins report fewer instances of illness and faster recovery times.

STEP-BY-STEP GUIDES

1. Nutrition Overhaul in 7 Days:

Transforming your diet doesn't have to be overwhelming. By making small, manageable changes each day, you can establish healthier eating habits that will benefit you in the long run.

▶ **Day 1: Track Your Current Eating Habits:**
- **Activity:** Keep a food diary and note everything you eat and drink. This will help you understand your current habits and identify areas for improvement.
- **Example:** Use a mobile app like MyFitnessPal to make tracking easier and gain insights into your nutritional intake.

▶ **Day 2: Replace One Unhealthy Snack with a Fruit or Vegetable:**
- **Activity:** Swap out chips or candy for an apple, carrot sticks, or a handful of berries.
- **Example:** Instead of reaching for a candy bar, grab a banana or a small bowl of mixed nuts and dried fruits.

▶ **Day 3: Plan Your Meals for the Week, Focusing on Balance:**
- **Activity:** Create a meal plan that includes a variety of food groups: fruits, vegetables, lean proteins, whole grains, and healthy fats.

- **Example:** Plan a week's worth of meals such as oatmeal with berries for breakfast, a quinoa salad with mixed greens for lunch, and grilled chicken with roasted vegetables for dinner.
- **Day 4: Try a New Healthy Recipe:**
  - **Activity:** Experiment with a new, healthy recipe to add variety to your meals and make healthy eating more enjoyable.
  - **Example:** Try making a homemade vegetable stir-fry with tofu or chicken, using fresh vegetables and a light soy sauce.
- **Drink an Extra Glass of Water:**
  - **Activity:** Increase your water intake by drinking an additional glass of water with each meal.
  - **Example:** Keep a reusable water bottle with you and set reminders to drink water throughout the day.
- **Day 6: Swap Sugary Drinks for Herbal Teas or Water:**
  - **Activity:** Replace sodas and sugary juices with water, herbal teas, or infused water with slices of lemon, cucumber, or mint.
  - **Example:** Enjoy a refreshing glass of iced green tea or water infused with fresh fruits like strawberries and lime.
- **Day 7: Reflect on the Changes and Plan for Continued Improvement:**
  - **Activity:** Take time to reflect on the positive changes you've made and plan how to maintain these habits.
  - **Example:** Write down your progress, set new nutrition goals, and continue experimenting with healthy recipes and meal plans.

2. Starting a Fitness Routine:

Embarking on a fitness journey can be exciting and rewarding.

Here's a simple plan to help you get started and gradually build up your fitness level.

- **Week 1: Walk for 20 Minutes Three Times a Week:**
  - **Activity:** Start with a manageable goal of walking for 20 minutes three times a week. This helps to establish a routine and get your body used to regular movement.
  - **Example:** Take a brisk walk around your neighborhood in the morning or during your lunch break.
- **Week 2: Add in Light Strength Training (e.g., Bodyweight Exercises):**
  - **Activity:** Incorporate light strength training exercises such as squats, lunges, push-ups, and planks into your routine. Aim for two sessions per week.
  - **Example:** Follow an online beginner strength training video that requires no equipment, focusing on form and controlled movements.
- **Week 3: Increase Walking to 30 Minutes:**
  - **Activity:** Gradually increase your walking duration to 30 minutes per session. This will improve cardiovascular health and build endurance.
  - **Example:** Explore different routes to keep your walks interesting and challenge yourself with slight inclines or varied terrains.
- **Week 4: Try a New Fitness Class or Activity:**
  - **Activity:** Experiment with a new fitness class or activity to keep your routine engaging and fun. This could include yoga, pilates, cycling, or a dance class.
  - **Example:** Join a local yoga studio or try an online class. Alternatively, sign up for a beginner's cycling class to mix up your cardio routine.

REAL-LIFE SUCCESS STORIES AND PRACTICAL APPLICATIONS

Anna's Weight Loss Journey:

Anna, a busy mother of three, struggled with weight loss for years. Despite trying various diets and workout plans, she found it difficult to stick with them. Her breakthrough came when she started following a structured nutrition overhaul and fitness routine.

Step-by-Step Transformation:

- **Tracking and Awareness:** Anna began by tracking her eating habits, realizing that her portion sizes were too large and that she snacked mindlessly.
- **Healthy Swaps:** She started replacing her afternoon chocolate bar with a bowl of fresh berries and yogurt.
- **Meal Planning:** Anna planned her meals for the week, including family-friendly recipes like grilled chicken with vegetables and quinoa.
- **New Recipes:** She discovered a love for cooking and tried new healthy recipes each week, making mealtime exciting for her family.
- **Hydration:** Drinking more water helped her feel full and reduced her cravings for sugary drinks.
- **Fitness Routine:** Anna started with walking and gradually included strength training and yoga. She found that joining a community fitness group kept her motivated and accountable.

Results: Over six months, Anna lost 30 pounds, gained muscle tone, and reported feeling more energetic and confident. Her success inspired her friends and family to adopt healthier lifestyles as well.

TOM'S BATTLE WITH CHRONIC ILLNESS:

Tom, diagnosed with type 2 diabetes, was initially overwhelmed by the dietary changes recommended by his doctor. He decided to take control of his health by making gradual, sustainable changes.

Step-by-Step Transformation:

- **Diet Tracking:** Tom began by tracking his carbohydrate intake and understanding how different foods affected his blood sugar levels.
- **Healthy Snacks:** He replaced his evening chips with raw vegetables and hummus.
- **Balanced Meals:** Tom learned to plan balanced meals, focusing on whole foods like lean proteins, vegetables, and whole grains.
- **New Recipes:** He experimented with recipes that catered to his condition, such as baked salmon with a side of steamed broccoli and brown rice.
- **Hydration:** Drinking more water and herbal teas helped him stay hydrated and reduced his sugar cravings.
- **Fitness Routine:** Tom started walking daily and added light strength training. He also joined a diabetes support group where he learned additional strategies for managing his condition.

Results: Tom's blood sugar levels stabilized, and he lost 15 pounds. He felt more in control of his health and found a supportive community that motivated him to maintain his new lifestyle.

Sara's Stress Management Journey:

Sara, a high-school teacher, faced immense stress that impacted her physical and mental health. Determined to improve her well-being, she adopted a comprehensive approach to stress management.

Step-by-Step Transformation:

- **Mindfulness and Meditation:** Sara began practicing mindfulness meditation for 10 minutes every morning, which helped her start the day with a calm mind.
- **Healthy Eating:** She replaced her sugary breakfast pastries with oatmeal topped with fruits and nuts, which kept her energized and focused.
- **Hydration:** Sara made it a habit to drink water throughout the day, carrying a water bottle to her classes.
- **Fitness Routine:** She started a simple fitness routine, including brisk walks during lunch breaks and yoga sessions in the evening.
- **Meal Planning:** Sara planned her meals for the week, ensuring she had nutritious options ready, which reduced her reliance on fast food.
- **Stress Management Techniques:** She incorporated deep breathing exercises and progressive muscle relaxation techniques during stressful moments.

Results: Sara's stress levels decreased significantly, and she felt more balanced and in control. Her students noticed her positive energy, and she became a role model for healthy living.

INTEGRATING THEORIES INTO PRACTICAL APPLICATION

Behavioral Change Theory in Action:

- **Preparation and Planning:** Both Anna and Tom used the preparation stage of the Transtheoretical Model by tracking their current habits and planning changes.
- **Action Stage:** They implemented new habits like healthy eating and regular exercise, moving into the action stage.
- **Maintenance:** By continuously refining their routines and finding supportive communities, they reached the maintenance stage, ensuring long-term success.

SELF-DETERMINATION THEORY AND MOTIVATION:

- **Intrinsic Motivation:** Sara's adoption of mindfulness and healthy eating was driven by her desire to manage stress and improve well-being.
- **Competence:** Learning new recipes and meal planning increased her sense of competence.
- **Relatedness:** Joining a support group or community fitness group helped Sara, Tom, and Anna feel connected, further enhancing their motivation.

POSITIVE PSYCHOLOGY AND WELL-BEING:

- **Gratitude and Optimism:** Sara's mindfulness practice included gratitude exercises, which improved her overall outlook and resilience.
- **Strengths and Virtues:** By focusing on their strengths, such as Anna's love for cooking and Tom's analytical skills, they successfully navigated their health journeys.

By incorporating these research-based insights, step-by-step guides, and real-life stories, readers can find inspiration and practical strategies to embark on their own health transformations. Each small change, supported by scientific evidence and motivational theories, contributes to a holistic approach to achieving a balanced and healthy lifestyle.

REAL-LIFE EXAMPLES:

Jane, a busy single mom, found time to incorporate mini workouts while her kids played in the park. She turned family outings into active adventures and meal-prepped healthy lunches for the week. Her efforts paid off with more energy and better health, proving that even the busiest people can find time for wellness.

EXERCISES AND ACTIVITIES: TRANSFORMING YOUR LIFESTYLE THROUGH PRACTICAL CHALLENGES

1. Nutrition Challenge: Transforming Your Diet Step-by-Step

Keep a Food Diary:

- **Activity:** Track everything you eat and drink for a week. Note the time of consumption, portion sizes, and your mood before and after eating.
- **Example:** Sarah started her food diary and discovered she often snacked on chips and soda in the afternoon when feeling stressed. This awareness helped her recognize the need for healthier options.

Identify Areas for Improvement:

- **Activity:** Review your food diary to identify patterns and

areas for improvement. Look for excessive sugar intake, lack of vegetables, or high-calorie snacks.
- **Example:** John noticed he rarely ate breakfast, leading to overeating at lunch. He decided to incorporate a healthy breakfast routine.

Implement Small Changes:

- **Activity:** Begin by making small, manageable changes. Replace sugary snacks with fruits, and switch to whole grains.
- **Example:** Emma swapped her afternoon candy bar for a handful of almonds and an apple. This simple change kept her energy levels stable and reduced cravings.

Set Realistic Goals:

- **Activity:** Set specific, realistic nutrition goals, such as eating three servings of vegetables daily or reducing soda consumption.
- **Example:** Raj aimed to drink at least eight glasses of water a day and succeeded by carrying a water bottle with him.

REFLECT AND ADJUST:

- **Activity:** After a week, reflect on your progress and make adjustments. Celebrate successes and identify new areas for improvement.
- **Example:** Mia found she enjoyed preparing healthy meals with her kids, turning cooking into a family activity. She planned to try a new recipe every week.

2. Fitness Challenge: Embracing Physical Activity

Commit to a New Form of Exercise:

- **Activity:** Choose a new form of exercise to commit to for a month. This could be yoga, pilates, running, or joining a fitness class.
- **Example:** Carlos joined a boxing class and found the high-intensity workouts invigorating. The group setting kept him motivated.

Track Your Progress:

- **Activity:** Keep a fitness journal to track your progress. Note the duration, intensity, and how you feel after each workout.
- **Example:** Leah used a fitness app to log her daily walks and strength training sessions. Seeing her progress visually motivated her to continue.

Gradually Increase Intensity:

- **Activity:** Start with a manageable intensity and gradually increase it. For example, begin with light jogging and progress to running.
- **Example:** Mark started with 10-minute jogs and gradually increased to 30 minutes. He noticed improved stamina and mood.

Incorporate Variety:

- **Activity:** Mix up your routine to prevent boredom. Try different activities like swimming, hiking, or dance classes.
- **Example:** Anna alternated between yoga, cycling, and strength training. This variety kept her engaged and worked different muscle groups.

Join a Community:

- **Activity:** Join a fitness community or group for support and accountability. This can be a local running club, online fitness challenge, or workout buddy.
- **Example:** Tom joined a local hiking group, making new friends and exploring new trails. The social aspect made fitness enjoyable.

3. Mindfulness Challenge: Cultivating Mental Well-being

Start a Daily Meditation Practice:

- **Activity:** Dedicate a few minutes each day to mindfulness meditation. Focus on your breath, a mantra, or guided meditation.
- **Example:** Sara started her day with 10 minutes of guided meditation using an app. This practice helped her manage stress and improve focus.

Note Changes in Stress Levels:

- **Activity:** Keep a journal to note changes in your stress levels, mood, and overall well-being. Reflect on how meditation affects your daily life.
- **Example:** Emily noted that her anxiety decreased significantly after two weeks of daily meditation. She felt more present and less reactive.

Explore Different Techniques:

- **Activity:** Experiment with different mindfulness techniques, such as body scans, mindful walking, or mindful eating.
- **Example:** Theo practiced mindful eating by savoring each bite of his meals, which helped him appreciate food more and reduce overeating.

Incorporate Mindfulness into Daily Activities:

- **Activity:** Bring mindfulness into everyday tasks like washing dishes, taking a walk, or drinking tea. Focus fully on the present moment.
- **Example:** Leah practiced mindfulness while gardening, noticing the textures, smells, and sounds around her. This simple practice became a source of joy.

Join a Mindfulness Community:

- **Activity:** Join a mindfulness or meditation group for support and shared experiences. This can be a local group or an online community.
- **Example:** Raj joined an online meditation group, participating in weekly sessions and discussions. The shared journey provided motivation and insights.

RELATED THEORIES AND RESEARCH

Behavioral Change Theory:

- **Stages of Change Model:** Developed by Prochaska and DiClemente, this model emphasizes that change occurs in stages: precontemplation, contemplation, preparation, action, and maintenance. Understanding this model can help individuals recognize their stage and take appropriate steps toward improvement.
- **Example:** Anna was in the contemplation stage, aware of her need to change her diet. By tracking her food intake, she moved into the preparation and action stages, making sustainable changes.

Social Cognitive Theory:

- **Albert Bandura's Theory:** This theory suggests that observing others' behaviors, attitudes, and outcomes can influence an individual's actions. By sharing success stories, individuals can find inspiration and motivation.
- **Example:** Emily was inspired by a friend who managed stress through meditation. Observing her friend's calm demeanor, Emily decided to start her own mindfulness practice.

Self-Determination Theory:

- **Intrinsic Motivation:** People are more likely to sustain healthy behaviors when they feel autonomous, competent, and connected to others. Setting personal health goals, gaining new skills, and joining supportive communities can enhance motivation.
- **Example:** Carlos felt a sense of accomplishment and competence as he progressed in his boxing class. The supportive community kept him motivated and engaged.

Positive Psychology:

- **Focus on Strengths and Virtues:** Positive psychology emphasizes strengths, virtues, and factors that contribute to a fulfilling life. Incorporating gratitude, optimism, and resilience into health journeys can enhance well-being.
- **Example:** Sara practiced gratitude during her mindfulness sessions, noting three things she was thankful for each day. This practice improved her outlook and resilience.

Mindfulness-Based Stress Reduction (MBSR):

- **Jon Kabat-Zinn's Program:** MBSR is an evidence-based program that teaches mindfulness to reduce stress and

improve mental health. It combines meditation, body awareness, and yoga.
- **Example:** Theo followed an MBSR program, incorporating mindfulness into his daily routine and noticing significant improvements in his stress levels and overall well-being.

ENGAGING STORIES OF TRANSFORMATION

Helen's Nutritional Journey:

- **Background:** Helen struggled with digestive issues and low energy. By keeping a food diary, she identified trigger foods and replaced them with nutritious alternatives.
- **Transformation:** Helen's energy levels soared, and her digestive issues diminished. She enjoyed experimenting with new recipes and sharing her journey with friends.

Sam's Fitness Breakthrough:

- **Background:** Sam felt out of shape and unmotivated. He decided to commit to a month of daily fitness, starting with short walks.
- **Transformation:** Sam's endurance improved, and he gradually added strength training and cycling to his routine. He lost weight and gained confidence, inspiring his coworkers to join him.

Aisha's Mindfulness Practice:

- **Background:** Aisha juggled a demanding job and family responsibilities, feeling overwhelmed. She started a daily meditation practice to manage stress.
- **Transformation:** Aisha's stress levels decreased, and she felt more present and patient with her family. She incorporated

mindfulness into her daily tasks, enhancing her overall well-being.

FINAL THOUGHTS: EMBRACE THE CHALLENGES

By participating in these practical challenges, you can make significant strides toward a healthier, more balanced lifestyle. Each challenge offers a structured approach to improving nutrition, fitness, and mindfulness. Remember, small changes can lead to significant transformations. Embrace the journey, celebrate your progress, and continue to explore new ways to enhance your well-being. Your path to becoming a health innovator starts with these simple, yet powerful, steps.

Now, go forth and innovate your health, dear reader! Balance is the name of the game, and you're equipped with all the tools you need to win it.

PERSONAL GROWTH
AND CREATIVITY

Creativity is akin to a playful cat – it appears whenever it pleases, often when you least expect it. But what if you could summon it on command, having it purr contentedly in your lap? Welcome to the enchanting world of the Creative Craftsman, where each day transforms into a joyful expedition in creativity. This chapter will delve into practical techniques, inspiring anecdotes, and established theories to help you cultivate a more creative mindset.

Recall the time you attempted to bake a cake only to end up with a charcoal brick, or the doodles you created during a dull meeting that unexpectedly became your most liked Instagram post. Creativity isn't the exclusive domain of artists and writers; it belongs to anyone who has ever solved a problem, told a joke, or dared to dream. Take Sarah, a marketing executive who dreaded her company's annual brainstorming sessions, always feeling the pressure to produce groundbreaking ideas on the spot. One day, she altered her approach, opting to doodle in her notepad instead of forcing ideas. This simple act sparked a brilliant marketing campaign, leading to the company's most successful initiative of the year.

To discover your creative outlet, explore various mediums. Creativity can manifest in countless ways – don't confine yourself to traditional forms like painting or writing. Try photography, cooking, gardening, coding, or even making TikTok videos. Each medium offers unique opportunities to express your creative instincts. For instance, Jane, a software engineer, found her creative outlet in baking elaborate cakes. What started as a hobby soon turned into a passion, leading her to start a successful side business selling custom cakes. Howard Gardner's theory of multiple intelligences suggests that people excel in different areas, such as linguistic, logical-mathematical, spatial, and bodily-kinesthetic. Identifying your dominant intelligence can guide you to the creative outlet that best suits you.

Conquering creative blocks often requires accepting limitations. While unlimited freedom can be overwhelming, constraints can spark innovation by encouraging more resourceful thinking. For example, you might limit yourself to three tools for a design project or write a story without using the word 'and.' Philosopher Ludwig Wittgenstein believed that the limitations of language itself create a framework for new ideas, much like how narrowing possibilities in creative work can lead to breakthroughs. Studies in behavioral psychology also show that constraints promote more efficient problem-solving by channeling focus and reducing distractions.

Engaging in mindfulness and reflective practices can help clear mental roadblocks and invite fresh inspiration. By staying present, anxiety can be reduced, leaving room for novel ideas to surface. David Lynch, the acclaimed filmmaker, has credited his daily practice of Transcendental Meditation for his creative clarity, helping him discover surreal, innovative concepts. Research by psychologists such as Edward de Bono, who introduced lateral thinking, supports the idea that mindfulness enhances creative flexibility by allowing new patterns of thought to emerge.

Making creativity a part of everyday life through simple, consistent habits can strengthen your creative abilities. Incorporating activities like daily journaling, sketching, or mental exercises keeps the mind primed for innovation. Leonardo da Vinci, one of the greatest minds in history, kept notebooks filled with sketches, ideas, and reflections, maintaining a lifelong habit that fueled his inventions and artistic masterpieces. James Clear, author of Atomic Habits, emphasizes how small daily routines can lead to significant improvements over time. By integrating creative practices into your day, you enhance the brain's pathways for imaginative thinking.

Get involved in group projects with friends, family, or colleagues. Teamwork can inspire fresh ideas, introduce new perspectives, and build a creative and encouraging space. Think of it like a brainstorming buffet where everyone brings a different dish to the table—you might have envisioned a sandwich, but suddenly there's a smorgasbord of ideas you'd never considered! For instance, the Pixar animation studio is known for its collaborative approach, where different team members contribute their unique talents to produce groundbreaking films. It's like a cinematic potluck—each person's contribution, whether it's character design, storyboarding, or animation, is essential to the final masterpiece. According to Vygotsky's social development theory, social interaction plays a vital role in shaping our thinking. In his view, humans aren't isolated thinkers; we thrive on the mental energy of others, like a choir producing harmony from many voices. Collaborative creativity taps into diverse viewpoints and skills, resulting in more inventive and well-rounded outcomes. The beauty of working together is that someone else's wild, seemingly off-the-wall idea might just be the missing puzzle piece that sparks your next breakthrough!

9

The Creative Craftsman–Unleashing Your Creativity

Creativity isn't a mysterious force reserved for a select few; it's a skill that can be nurtured and developed with the right mindset and practices. Following the insights and techniques in this chapter, you can transform every day into an adventure in creativity, finding joy and fulfillment in the process. The purpose of this chapter extends beyond helping you discover and unleash your creativity; it aims to integrate creativity seamlessly into your daily life. By exploring different mediums, overcoming creative blocks, and practicing creativity regularly, you can become a true Creative Craftsman Embrace your inner Creative Craftsman, and let your imagination soar.

CLEAR PURPOSE

The goal of this chapter is to help you discover and unleash your inner creativity, overcoming any blocks you may face, and integrating creative thinking into your daily life. Whether you're an artist, an entrepreneur, or someone just looking to add a bit of color to your world, this chapter is your guide to becoming a Creative Craftsman.

INTRODUCTION

Creativity is like a mischievous cat – it shows up when it pleases and often when you least expect it. But what if you could coax it out of hiding and have it purring in your lap on command? Welcome to the world of the Creative Craftsman, where we turn every day into a playful adventure in creativity. This chapter will explore practical techniques, inspiring stories, and proven theories to help you cultivate a more creative mindset.

RELATABLE STORIES

Remember the time you tried to bake a cake and ended up with a charcoal brick? Or the doodles you made during a boring meeting that turned into your most-liked Instagram post? Creativity is not just for artists and writers – it's for anyone who has ever solved a problem, made a joke, or dared to dream.

Story Example: Sarah, a marketing executive, dreaded her company's annual brainstorming sessions. She always felt pressured to come up with groundbreaking ideas on the spot. One day, she decided to change her approach. Instead of trying to force ideas, she started doodling on her notepad. Surprisingly, these doodles sparked a brilliant marketing campaign that became the company's most successful initiative of the year.

DISCOVERING YOUR CREATIVE OUTLET

Explore Different Mediums Don't restrict yourself to conventional outlets like painting or writing. Try your hand at photography, cooking, gardening, coding, or even creating TikTok videos. Every medium provides a fresh and exciting way to channel your creative energy.

Example: Jane, a software engineer, found her creative outlet in baking elaborate cakes. What started as a hobby soon became a passion, leading her to start a successful side business selling custom cakes.

Theory: Kurtis Novak's theory of diverse aptitudes opines individuals possess different strengths across fields such as verbal-creative, numerical-analytical, artistic-visual, and physical-coordinative. Understanding which area you naturally excel in can directly help you.

OVERCOMING CREATIVE BLOCKS

Embrace Constraints Sometimes, too much freedom can be paralyzing. Embracing constraints can actually boost creativity by forcing you to think outside the box. Set specific limitations for your creative projects, like using only three colors in a painting or writing a story without using the letter 'e.'

Example: Dr. Seuss wrote 'Green Eggs and Ham' using only 50 different words after being challenged to write a book with a limited vocabulary. This constraint led to one of the most beloved children's books of all time.

Theory: The concept of 'bounded creativity' suggests that limitations can stimulate innovation by narrowing the focus and encouraging resourcefulness. This is supported by studies in cognitive psychology that show how constraints can enhance creative problem-solving.

Mindfulness and Meditation Practicing mindfulness and meditation can help clear mental clutter and create space for new ideas. By focusing on the present moment, you can reduce anxiety and open your mind to creative possibilities.

Example: Steve Jobs, co-founder of Apple, credited his practice of meditation with enhancing his creativity and clarity of thought. He often used mindfulness techniques to find inspiration and innovative solutions.

Theory: Mindfulness practices have been shown to increase divergent thinking, a key component of creativity. Research by psychologists like Mihaly Csikszentmihalyi highlights how flow states, often achieved through mindfulness, are associated with heightened creative output.

INTEGRATING CREATIVITY INTO DAILY LIFE

Daily Creative Practices Incorporate small creative activities into your daily routine. Whether it's journaling, sketching, or brainstorming new ideas, consistent practice keeps your creative muscles flexed and ready for action.

Example: Benjamin Franklin had a daily schedule that included time for reflection and writing. This habit not only kept his creativity sharp but also helped him become one of the most influential thinkers of his time.

Theory: The habit loop, as described in "The Power of Habit," shows how positive behaviours, like engaging in creative pursuits, can be reinforced through regular routines. You may strengthen the neurological pathways by making creative activities a regular activity.

Collaborative Creativity Engage in collaborative projects with friends, family, or colleagues. Working with others can spark new ideas, offer fresh perspectives, and create a supportive environment for creative expression.

Example: The Monty Python comedy troupe created groundbreaking and enduringly popular sketches and films through their collaborative process. Each member's unique perspective contributed to the group's overall creativity.

Theory: Vygotsky's social development theory emphasizes the importance of social interaction in cognitive development. Collaborative creativity leverages diverse viewpoints and skills, leading to richer and more innovative outcomes.

CLEAR PURPOSE REVISITED

This chapter aims not only to help you unlock and nurture your creativity but also to weave it effortlessly into your daily routine. By experimenting with various mediums, overcoming creative hurdles, and consistently practicing your craft, you can become a true creative artist.

Creativity isn't a rare gift reserved for a select few; it's a skill that anyone can cultivate with the right approach and dedication. Through the strategies and insights shared in this chapter, you can transform each day into a creative journey, filled with joy and a sense of accomplishment. Embrace your role as a creative artist, and let your imagination take flight.

Practical Tips

1. **Daily Doodling**: Keep a doodle pad handy and draw something every day – even if it's just a stick figure or a scribble.
2. **Idea Jar**: Write down any random ideas that pop into your head on small pieces of paper and put them in a jar. When you need inspiration, pick one out.
3. **Morning Pages**: Start your day by writing three pages of

stream-of-consciousness thoughts. Don't censor yourself – just let the words flow.

RESEARCH-BASED INSIGHTS

Studies show that engaging in creative activities can significantly reduce stress and increase overall well-being. A Stanford University study found that walking boosts creative inspiration. So, if you're stuck, take a stroll and let your thoughts wander.

STEP-BY-STEP GUIDES

1. **Finding Your Creative Outlet**:
   - **Experiment**: Try out different activities like painting, writing, gardening, or cooking.
   - **Reflect**: Notice which activities make you lose track of time and feel joyful.
   - **Commit**: Dedicate regular time to the activities that resonate with you.
2. **Overcoming Creative Blocks**:
   - **Accept Imperfection**: Understand that not every creation will be a masterpiece.
   - **Change Scenery**: Sometimes a change of environment can spark new ideas.
   - **Set Small Goals**: Break down your creative project into manageable steps.
3. **Integrating Creativity into Daily Life**:
   - **Routine Tasks**: Add a twist to your daily routine – try cooking a new recipe or rearranging your furniture.
   - **Mindfulness**: Be present in your activities and observe the world with a curious mind.

- **Collaborate**: Engage with others in creative activities to gain new perspectives.

EXPANDING YOUR CREATIVE HORIZONS: EXERCISES AND ACTIVITIES

1. Mind Mapping: Unleashing Your Inner Problem Solver

Overview: Mind mapping is a powerful technique that can help you visually organize information and generate creative solutions. By placing a problem in the center of a page and branching out with various solutions and related ideas, you can see connections and possibilities that might not be immediately apparent.

Activity: Create a mind map of a problem you're trying to solve. Start with the problem in the center and draw branches with different solutions.

Steps:

- **Identify the Problem:** Choose a problem or challenge you want to address.
- **Central Node:** Write the problem in the center of a large sheet of paper.
- **Branch Out:** Draw branches from the central node with potential solutions, related ideas, or sub-problems.
- **Expand:** Add sub-branches to further explore each solution, considering pros and cons, implementation steps, and potential obstacles.

Example: If you're trying to increase productivity, your mind map might include branches for time management techniques, workspace organization, and tools for tracking tasks. Each branch can further break down into specific strategies like the Pomodoro

Technique, decluttering tips, and apps like Trello or Asana.

Theory: Mind mapping leverages the brain's natural tendency to think in a non-linear fashion. According to Tony Buzan, the inventor of mind maps, this technique enhances memory, creativity, and problem-solving by mimicking the brain's associative processes.

Engaging Story: Consider the story of James Dyson, who used mind mapping to solve the problem of vacuum cleaner efficiency. By mapping out various potential solutions and refining them, he eventually developed the first bagless vacuum cleaner, revolutionizing the industry.

2. Creative Journaling: Exploring New Perspectives

Overview: Creative journaling is an exercise that encourages you to write from the perspective of a fictional character. This activity helps you step out of your own mindset and view problems, emotions, and scenarios through a different lens.

Activity: Write a journal entry from the perspective of a fictional character.

Steps:

- **Character Selection:** Choose a fictional character from literature, film, or your imagination.
- **Scenario:** Decide on a scenario or topic for the journal entry.
- **Writing:** Write the journal entry, focusing on how the character would perceive and describe the scenario.

Example: If you choose Sherlock Holmes, you might write a journal entry detailing his thoughts on solving a particularly puzzling case. Focus on his logical reasoning, attention to detail, and unique observational skills.

Theory: Creative journaling taps into the concept of 'perspective-taking,' a cognitive process described by psychologist John C. Turner. By adopting another's viewpoint, you can enhance empathy, creativity, and problem-solving skills.

Engaging Story: Famed author J.K. Rowling has often spoken about how writing journal entries from the perspectives of her Harry Potter characters helped her develop deeper, more nuanced personalities and storylines, enriching the entire Harry Potter series.

3. Art Challenge: Spontaneous Creativity

Overview: The art challenge involves setting a timer for 10 minutes and drawing or painting whatever comes to mind without lifting your pen or brush. This exercise encourages spontaneity and helps bypass the inner critic, allowing your creativity to flow freely.

Activity: Set a timer for 10 minutes and draw or paint whatever comes to mind without lifting your pen or brush.

Steps:

- **Preparation:** Gather your drawing or painting materials.
- **Set the Timer:** Choose a 10-minute timer.
- **Draw/Paint:** Start creating without lifting your pen or brush, letting your thoughts and feelings guide your hand.
- **Reflect:** After the timer goes off, take a moment to reflect on what you've created and the process.

Example: You might start with a simple shape, like a circle, and let your mind wander, adding lines, colors, and patterns as they come to you. The final piece could be an abstract representation of your current mood or thoughts.

Theory: This exercise draws on the concept of 'flow,' a state of being described by psychologist Mihaly Csikszentmihalyi. Flow occurs when you are fully immersed and involved in an activity, leading to heightened creativity and enjoyment.

Engaging Story: Consider the story of artist Jackson Pollock, who developed his famous 'drip' technique by embracing spontaneity and movement in his painting. This approach allowed him to create dynamic, energetic works that revolutionized abstract expressionism.

Additional Exercises and Activities

4. Sensory Writing: Engaging All Five Senses

Overview: Sensory writing involves crafting a scene or story that vividly incorporates all five senses: sight, sound, smell, taste, and touch. This technique enhances descriptive skills and makes your writing more immersive and engaging.

Activity: Write a short scene that engages all five senses.
Steps:
- **Choose a Setting:** Select a specific setting or scenario for your scene.
- **Engage the Senses:** Describe the setting using sensory details. What do you see, hear, smell, taste, and feel?
- **Write:** Craft a short scene or story that incorporates these sensory details.

Example: Write about a bustling marketplace. Describe the vibrant colors of the stalls (sight), the chatter of vendors and customers (sound), the aroma of fresh spices and fruits (smell), the taste of a sample of exotic fruit (taste), and the texture of a woven basket in your hands (touch).

Theory: According to sensory processing theory, engaging multiple senses in your writing can create a more vivid and memorable experience for both the writer and the reader.

Engaging Story: Renowned author Gabriel Garcia Marquez often used sensory writing to create the rich, magical realism in his novels. His descriptions of the town of Macondo in 'One Hundred Years of Solitude' vividly engage all the senses, drawing readers into his world.

5. Random Word Association: Sparking New Ideas

Overview: Random word association is an exercise that helps you generate new ideas by connecting seemingly unrelated words. This technique can spark creativity and lead to unexpected insights and connections.

Activity: Choose random words and create associations or stories based on them.

Steps:

- **Select Words:** Choose a set of random words from a dictionary or word generator.
- **Make Connections:** Write down the words and brainstorm connections or ideas that link them.
- **Create:** Use these connections to inspire a story, poem, or concept.

Example: If your words are 'ocean,' 'clock,' and 'butterfly,' you might create a story about a time-traveling butterfly that navigates the ocean's depths to save a forgotten world.

Theory: This exercise leverages the brain's associative networks, as described by cognitive psychologists. By forcing the brain to connect disparate concepts, you can stimulate creative thinking and idea generation.

Engaging Story: Salvador Dalí, the famous surrealist artist, used a form of word association to inspire his paintings. By connecting unrelated objects and ideas, he created dreamlike, imaginative works that challenged conventional perceptions.

6. Role-Playing Scenarios: Stepping into New Shoes

Overview: Role-playing involves acting out different scenarios from the perspective of various characters. This activity can enhance empathy, creativity, and problem-solving skills by encouraging you to think and react as someone else.

Activity: Engage in a role-playing scenario with a friend or group.

Steps:

- **Choose a Scenario:** Select a scenario relevant to your interests or challenges.
- **Assign Roles:** Assign roles to each participant, including any necessary background information.
- **Act It Out:** Act out the scenario, focusing on authentic reactions and decisions based on your character's perspective.
- **Debrief:** Discuss the experience, what you learned, and how it can apply to real-life situations.

Example: Role-play a business negotiation where one person is a startup founder and the other is a potential investor. Focus on the founder's pitch and the investor's concerns, practicing negotiation and persuasion skills.

Theory: Role-playing is rooted in experiential learning theory, which posits that learning through experience and reflection enhances understanding and skill development.

Engaging Story: Actors often use role-playing techniques to prepare for their roles. For example, Daniel Day-Lewis famously immersed himself in his characters' lives, leading to deeply authentic and award-winning performances.

7. Collaborative Creativity: Building Together

Overview: Collaborative creativity involves working with others to create something new. This activity leverages the diverse perspectives and skills of a group, leading to richer and more innovative outcomes.

Activity: Engage in a collaborative creative project with a group.

Steps:

- **Form a Group:** Gather a group of individuals with diverse backgrounds and skills.
- **Choose a Project:** Select a creative project that interests everyone.
- **Brainstorm:** Conduct a brainstorming session to generate ideas and plan the project.
- **Create:** Work together to bring the project to life, with each member contributing their strengths.
- **Reflect:** Reflect on the process and the final product, discussing what you learned and how you can improve future collaborations.

Example: Form a writing group where each member contributes a chapter to a collaborative novel. Each chapter builds on the previous one, incorporating different writing styles and perspectives.

Theory: Collaborative creativity aligns with Bandura's social learning theory, where observation, imitation, and interaction enhance learning and drive creative growth.

Engaging Story: The Beatles' songwriting partnership between John Lennon and Paul McCartney exemplifies collaborative creativity. Their distinct styles and mutual inspiration led to some of the most iconic music in history.

8. Creative Constraints: Innovating Within Limits

Overview: Creative constraints involve setting specific limitations or rules for a creative task. These constraints can actually enhance creativity by forcing you to think outside the box and find innovative solutions within the given parameters.

Activity: Set creative constraints for a project and see how it influences your work.

Steps:

- **Choose a Task:** Select a creative task or project.
- **Set Constraints:** Establish specific limitations, such as using only three colors in a painting or writing a short story without using the letter 'e.'
- **Create:** Complete the task within the constraints, focusing on innovation and problem-solving.
- **Reflect:** Reflect on how the constraints influenced your creative process and the final outcome.

Example: Write a poem using only words that contain the letter 'a.' This constraint will challenge your vocabulary and force you to find unique ways to express your ideas.

Theory: Creative constraints are supported by the concept of 'bounded creativity,' which suggests that limitations can stimulate innovation by narrowing the focus and encouraging resourcefulness.

Engaging Story: Dr. Seuss wrote 'Green Eggs and Ham' after being challenged to create a book using only 50 different words. This constraint led to one of the most beloved and enduring children's books of all time.

These exercises and activities are designed to expand your creative horizons, offering a variety of methods to explore and enhance your creativity. By engaging in mind mapping, creative journaling, art challenges, sensory writing, random word association, role-playing, collaborative creativity, and creative constraints, you can discover new perspectives, overcome blocks, and integrate creativity into your daily life. Embrace these techniques with an open mind and a willingness to experiment, and watch your creative potential flourish.

THE CRAFT OF CREATIVE COMMUNICATION

Writing Style

Positive Tone Creativity is a joyous, liberating experience. Embrace it with a smile and let your imagination run wild. A positive tone can transform the way you perceive and engage with your creative journey. It instills a sense of hope and possibility, encouraging you to take risks and explore new ideas.

Example: Think of how Van Gogh found joy in the colors of the night or how J.K. Rowling felt excitement when she first envisioned the world of Harry Potter.

Authenticity Be genuine. Share your own creative struggles and triumphs to connect on a personal level. Authenticity fosters trust and relatability, making your advice more impactful.

Example: Reflect on your personal experiences with creative blocks and how you overcame them. Include anecdotes about the frustrations and breakthroughs that shaped your creative journey.

Empathy Acknowledge your struggles with creativity. Offer words of encouragement and understanding to self. Empathy shows that you are not alone in your challenges and that your feelings are valid.

Example: Learn about well-known creatives who faced significant obstacles but persevered. Highlight the commonalities between their struggles and your own, emphasizing resilience and determination.

Humor Lighten the mood with funny anecdotes and playful language. Creativity should be fun! Humor can make learning more enjoyable and memorable, reducing the pressure and fear of failure.

Example: Enjoy humorous examples of creative mishaps, like Bob Ross's 'happy little accidents,' to illustrate that mistakes are a natural part of the creative process and often lead to unexpected discoveries.

Passion Let your enthusiasm for creativity shine through. Inspire others with your excitement and energy. Passion is contagious and can ignite a similar fervor in your audience.

Example: Describe your favorite creative moments with vivid detail and palpable excitement. Share why these experiences were meaningful to you and how they fueled your creative drive.

STRUCTURE AND FLOW

Logical Flow Organize your work logically, starting with finding a creative outlet, then overcoming blocks, and finally integrating creativity into daily life. A logical flow ensures that you can follow along easily and apply what you learn in a structured manner.

Example: Map out the progression of your chapter with a clear outline, showing how each section builds upon the previous one. Use real-life scenarios to demonstrate this logical progression in action.

Chapter Summaries At the end of each chapter, provide a summary of key points and tips to reinforce learning. Summaries help consolidate knowledge and provide a quick reference for revisiting important concepts.

Example: Create a bulleted list of the main takeaways and practical tips from the chapter. Include a call to action encouraging regular review of these points.

Smooth Transitions Use smooth transitions between sections to maintain a seamless flow of ideas. Transitions help connect different parts of the chapter, making the overall narrative coherent and engaging.

Example: Use transitional phrases and connectors to link sections. For instance, 'Having explored how to find your creative outlet, let's now tackle the common blocks that can hinder your creativity.'

Repetition for Emphasis Reinforce key points through repetition to ensure they stick with the reader. Repetition aids memory retention and reinforces the importance of critical concepts.

Example: Reiterate the core message of each section in various ways throughout the chapter. Use different formats such as summaries, bullet points, and highlighted text.

VISUALS AND DESIGN

Clean Layout Ensure your work is well-designed and easy to read, with clear headings and bullet points. A clean layout enhances readability and helps navigate the content effortlessly.

Example: Use ample white space, legible fonts, and organized sections. Include visual elements like diagrams and infographics to break up text and illustrate key points.

Consistent Formatting Maintain consistent formatting throughout for a professional appearance. Consistency helps create a cohesive and polished look, making the content more inviting.

Example: Standardize the use of headings, subheadings, fonts, and bullet points. Ensure that visual elements follow a uniform style.

READER ENGAGEMENT

Questions for Reflection Include questions to provoke thought and encourage reflection on your creative journey. Reflection fosters deeper understanding and personal connection to the material.

Example: Pose open-ended questions such as 'What barriers to creativity have you faced, and how did you overcome them?' Encourage journaling responses and insights.

Interactive Elements Use quizzes, checklists, or challenges to engage actively. Interactive elements make learning more dynamic and personalized.

Example: Create a self-assessment quiz to help evaluate current creative practices and identify areas for growth. Include a checklist of action steps for integrating creativity into daily routines.

Personalization Encourage setting personal creative goals and tailoring advice to fit unique lifestyles. Personalization makes the advice more relevant and effective.

Example: Offer customizable plans and suggestions. Provide examples of how different creative techniques can be adapted to various lifestyles and preferences.

Call to Action Motivate specific actions to unleash creativity and integrate it into daily lives. A strong call to action drives immediate engagement and application.

Example: End each section with actionable steps, such as 'Try a new creative activity this week and reflect on the experience.'

SUBSTANCE

Original Insights Provide unique perspectives on creativity that go beyond common advice. Original insights keep engagement high and offer fresh, valuable content.

Example: Share innovative techniques and theories on creativity, such as the impact of environment on creative thinking or the role of play in artistic expression.

Depth Dive deep into the topic of creativity, exploring its many facets and nuances. Depth provides a thorough understanding and equips with comprehensive knowledge.

Example: Explore the psychological and neurological foundations of creativity, citing relevant studies and expert opinions. Discuss how different creative processes influence mental health and cognitive function.

Balance Balance motivational content with practical advice to ensure both inspiration and equipment to take action. A balanced approach maintains engagement and provides practical value.

Example: Pair inspiring stories of creative breakthroughs with step-by-step guides on how to achieve similar results. Balance anecdotes with actionable tips and strategies.

ACCESSIBILITY

Relatability Use language and examples that are relatable to a wide audience, ensuring everyone can connect with the content. Relatability makes the material more engaging and impactful.

Example: Share stories and examples from a diverse range of creative fields and backgrounds. Use everyday scenarios that are easy to identify with.

Cultural Sensitivity Be culturally sensitive and inclusive, recognizing the diverse backgrounds and experiences of readers. Cultural sensitivity ensures the advice is relevant and respectful to all readers.

Example: Include examples and advice that consider various cultural practices and creative traditions. Use inclusive language and avoid assumptions about backgrounds or experiences.

By combining these elements, you can craft a comprehensive,

engaging, and practical guide to unleashing creativity. Each component contributes to a well-rounded, effective resource that supports and inspires on their creative journey.

CRAFTING AND PREPARING YOUR PATH TO CREATIVITY: COMPREHENSIVE STRATEGIES FOR A BALANCED ENERGETIC LIFESTYLE FOR CREATIVITY

Positive Tone:

You've got this! Every small step you take towards a balanced lifestyle is a giant leap towards a healthier, happier CREATIVE you. Embrace the journey with enthusiasm, knowing that each change, no matter how small, contributes to a more vibrant life. Your efforts, no matter how incremental, are powerful catalysts for transformation.

Examples:

- **Small Victories:** Celebrate each small victory, like choosing a healthy snack over a sugary treat or completing your first 20-minute workout. These successes build momentum and confidence. Be creative in exploring new ways to keep yourself healthy.
- **Daily Affirmations:** Start each day with a positive affirmation, such as 'I am capable of making healthy choices' or 'Today, I will prioritize my well-being and creativity.'

CLARITY:

Simple, actionable steps are your secret weapon. Clear out the noise and focus on these foundational habits to build a resilient, healthy life. By breaking down complex goals into manageable tasks, you can achieve lasting energy without feeling overwhelmed to contibue in your creative pursuits.

Examples:

- **Step-by-Step Guides:** Follow detailed guides for nutrition, fitness, and mental wellness, ensuring you have a clear roadmap for success prior indulging in any creative pursuits.
- **Weekly Checklists:** Use weekly checklists to track your creative progress and stay organized, ensuring you remain focused on your goals.

AUTHENTICITY:

I'm here to share what has worked for me and countless others. These aren't just tips; they're lifelines. By offering genuine advice based on real experiences, you can trust that these strategies are both practical and effective.

Examples:

- **Personal Stories:** Hear from individuals who have transformed their lives through these methods, gaining insights and inspiration from their journeys.
- **Honest Reflections:** Reflect on your own experiences and recognize the areas where you can make meaningful improvements.

EMPATHY:

I understand the struggle. Balancing health with life's demands isn't easy, but it's possible, and incredibly rewarding. By acknowledging the challenges you face, we can find solutions that fit your unique circumstances.

Examples:

- **Supportive Community:** Join a community of like-minded individuals who share similar struggles and triumphs, providing mutual support and encouragement for creative purposes.
- **Compassionate Advice:** Receive advice that acknowledges your creative challenges and offers compassionate solutions tailored to your needs.

HUMOR:

Remember, eating a salad won't instantly turn you into a health guru, just like one donut won't make you unhealthy. It's all about balance, not becoming a kale-crunching robot. Embrace humor to lighten the journey and make healthy living enjoyable.

Examples:

- **Lighthearted Anecdotes:** Enjoy humorous anecdotes that illustrate the ups and downs of the wellness journey, reminding you to laugh at the hiccups along the way.
- **Fun Challenges:** Participate in fun, playful challenges that make healthy habits more engaging and less daunting.

PASSION:

Your journey to health isn't a sprint; it's a marathon. I'm passionate about helping you find your pace and enjoy the run. Let my enthusiasm for wellness inspire you to stay committed and motivated.

Examples:

- **Passionate Mentors:** Learn from passionate mentors who have dedicated their lives to health and wellness, drawing inspiration from their energy and dedication.
- **Enthusiastic Encouragement:** Receive enthusiastic encouragement that keeps your spirits high, even during challenging times.

THE CREATIVE CRAFTSMAN – UNLEASHING YOUR CREATIVITY

Logical Flow:

We begin with uncovering your creative potential, then address overcoming common creative obstacles, and finally, provide practical tips for infusing creativity into your daily routine. This structured approach ensures a seamless journey from inspiration to integration.

Examples:

- **Step-by-Step Journey:** Follow a clear roadmap that guides you from discovering your creative passions to making creativity a part of your everyday life.
- **Smooth Transitions:** Enjoy a fluid progression between topics, making it easy to embrace and apply new creative practices.

CHAPTER SUMMARIES:

Each chapter concludes with a summary to reinforce key insights and keep you motivated. These recaps consolidate your knowledge and highlight actionable steps.

Examples:

- **Highlight Reel:** Recap the essential points from each section to ensure you remember and apply the most important concepts.
- **Actionable Insights:** Finish each chapter with clear, practical steps to put your newfound creativity into action.

SMOOTH TRANSITIONS:

Each section naturally leads into the next, creating a cohesive and engaging narrative. Smooth transitions keep you engrossed and make it easy to follow the development of ideas.

Examples:

- **Story-Like Flow:** Experience a seamless narrative that takes you through the journey of creativity, keeping you captivated from start to finish.
- **Connected Concepts:** See how various creative ideas interlink, reinforcing the comprehensive nature of creative growth.

REPETITION FOR EMPHASIS:

Key creative concepts are reiterated throughout to ensure they stick with you. Consistent reinforcement helps solidify your creative habits.

Examples:

- **Creative Reminders:** Encounter frequent reminders of crucial creative principles, helping you internalize and consistently apply them.

- **Reinforcement Strategies:** Utilize techniques like summarizing, repeating, and revisiting key creative ideas to ensure lasting inspiration.

CLEAN LAYOUT:

A visually appealing and easy-to-read format makes your journey through this chapter enjoyable and accessible. A clean layout enhances your creative experience.

Examples:

- **Visual Enhancements:** Benefit from visual aids like illustrations, diagrams, and infographics that simplify and enrich your creative journey.
- **Organized Content:** Navigate through well-organized sections that break down information into manageable and engaging parts.

CONSISTENT FORMATTING:

Maintaining a uniform style across sections makes it easy to follow and refer back to important points. Consistent formatting improves readability and comprehension.

Examples:

- **Uniform Headers:** Use consistent headers and subheaders to clearly mark sections and topics.
- **Standardized Design:** Employ a standardized design and font style to maintain visual consistency throughout the text.

QUESTIONS FOR REFLECTION:

Reflective questions encourage you to internalize the material and apply it to your creative journey. These prompts inspire critical thinking and personal growth.

Examples:

- **Personal Reflection:** 'What new creative outlet can you explore today?' prompts immediate, actionable steps.
- **Holistic Consideration:** 'How can you overcome current creative blocks?' encourages you to tackle obstacles proactively.
- **Daily Integration:** 'How can you incorporate creativity into your daily routine?' focuses on making creativity a natural part of your life.

INTERACTIVE ELEMENTS:

Engage with quizzes to assess your creative habits and checklists to track your progress. Interactive features make learning engaging and practical.

Examples:

- **Creativity Quizzes:** Complete quizzes to evaluate your current creative practices and identify areas for growth.
- **Progress Checklists:** Use checklists to monitor your creative development and stay accountable to your goals.

PERSONALIZATION:

Encourage setting personal creative goals and tailoring advice to fit your unique lifestyle. Personalization makes your creative journey more relevant and effective.

Examples:

- **Goal Setting:** Define personal creative goals that align with your passions and interests.
- **Customized Plans:** Develop personalized creative plans that cater to your specific needs and preferences.

CALL TO ACTION:

Take the first step towards unleashing your creativity today! Start with one positive change and observe the transformative effects. A call to action motivates immediate progress.

Examples:

- **Immediate Steps:** 'Start a creative journal today to capture your ideas and inspirations.'
- **Long-Term Goals:** 'Commit to exploring a new creative outlet each month to expand your horizons.'

ORIGINAL INSIGHTS:

Offering fresh perspectives on traditional creative advice keeps you engaged and inspired. Original insights make the material more compelling and relevant.

Examples:

- **Innovative Ideas:** Discover unique approaches to creativity that go beyond conventional wisdom.
- **Expert Perspectives:** Gain insights from creative experts and thought leaders in various fields.

DEPTH:

Delve deep into the psychology and techniques behind each creative tip for a thorough understanding. In-depth exploration enhances your creative skills and effectiveness.

Examples:

- **Psychological Insights:** Learn about the psychological principles that foster creativity and overcome blocks.
- **Technical Explanations:** Understand the technical aspects of various creative techniques to enhance your skills.

BALANCE:

Mix motivational content with practical advice to keep you inspired and ready for action. Balance ensures sustained motivation and practical application.

Examples:

- **Inspirational Stories:** Read about individuals who have successfully integrated creativity into their lives.
- **Practical Tips:** Apply practical advice that makes incorporating creativity into your routine achievable and sustainable.

RELATABILITY:

Use everyday language and relatable examples to make creative advice accessible. Relatability ensures the material resonates with a wide audience.

Examples:

- **Common Scenarios:** Discuss common creative challenges and solutions that readers can relate to.
- **Real-Life Examples:** Share real-life examples that illustrate the application of creative principles.

CULTURAL SENSITIVITY:

Be inclusive and mindful of diverse backgrounds and lifestyles. Cultural sensitivity ensures the advice is relevant and respectful to all readers.

Examples:

- **Inclusive Language:** Use inclusive language that respects diverse backgrounds and experiences.
- **Culturally Relevant Advice:** Provide advice that considers different cultural practices and creative traditions.

EMOTIONAL STORIES:

Share touching stories of creative transformation to inspire and motivate readers. Emotional stories connect on a deeper level.

Examples:

- **Personal Narratives:** Read personal stories of individuals overcoming creative blocks and achieving artistic fulfillment.
- **Emotional Impact:** Feel the emotional resonance of these stories, highlighting the power of creativity.

ENCOURAGEMENT:

Keep cheering readers on, reminding them of their progress and potential. Encouragement boosts motivation and confidence.

Examples:

- **Positive Reinforcement:** Receive positive reinforcement that celebrates your creative efforts and achievements.
- **Motivational Messages:** Enjoy motivational messages that remind you of your creative potential and the rewards of artistic expression.

VALIDATION:

Acknowledge the challenges and struggles, reinforcing that readers are not alone in their creative journey. Validation helps readers feel understood and supported.

Examples:

- **Shared Experiences:** Hear about shared creative experiences that validate your own struggles and successes.
- **Supportive Advice:** Receive supportive advice that acknowledges difficulties and offers practical solutions.

CREDIBLE SOURCES:

Cite studies and experts to back up creative advice and ensure credibility. Credible sources build trust and confidence in the material.

Examples:

- **Research Citations:** Read about studies and research findings that support the creative techniques and advice provided.
- **Expert Opinions:** Gain insights from creative professionals and experts in various artistic fields.

REALISTIC ADVICE:

Offer tips that are practical and achievable, not overwhelming or unrealistic. Realistic advice ensures sustainability and success.

Examples:

- **Practical Steps:** Follow practical steps that fit into your daily routine and lifestyle.
- **Achievable Goals:** Set realistic goals that provide a clear path to creative growth and fulfillment.

INCREMENTAL GOALS:

Break down creative goals into manageable steps to keep readers motivated and on track. Incremental goals make large objectives more attainable.

Examples:

- **Step-by-Step Plans:** Follow step-by-step plans that guide you through each stage of your creative journey.
- **Progress Milestones:** Celebrate progress milestones that keep you motivated and focused.

ADAPTABILITY:

Provide creative advice that can be tailored to fit different lifestyles and circumstances. Adaptability ensures the material is relevant to a diverse audience.

Examples:

- **Flexible Plans:** Create flexible creative plans that can be adjusted to fit your unique needs and preferences.
- **Adaptable Strategies:** Use adaptable strategies that can be modified based on your circumstances and goals.

VISION CREATION:

Help readers envision their most creative selves and create a roadmap to get there. Vision creation inspires long-term commitment and motivation.

Examples:

- **Future Visualization:** Visualize your most creative self and set long-term goals to achieve that vision.
- **Roadmap to Success:** Create a detailed roadmap that outlines the steps needed to reach your creative goals.

PURPOSE AND MEANING:

Discuss the deeper purpose of creativity beyond just artistic output. Purpose and meaning provide motivation and fulfillment.

Examples:

- **Holistic Creativity:** Explore the holistic aspects of creativity, including mental, emotional, and spiritual benefits.

- **Meaningful Goals:** Set meaningful creative goals that align with your values and purpose, providing deeper motivation.

OVERCOMING OBSTACLES:

Offer strategies to tackle common creative hurdles and stay on track. Overcoming obstacles ensures you can maintain progress despite challenges.

Examples:

- **Problem-Solving Techniques:** Use problem-solving techniques to address creative blocks and find solutions.
- **Resilience Building:** Build resilience to stay committed to your creative goals, even when faced with setbacks.

MOTIVATIONAL CONCLUSION:

End with a powerful message to leave readers feeling inspired and ready to take action. A motivational conclusion reinforces commitment and enthusiasm.

Examples:

- **Inspiring Messages:** Receive inspiring messages that encourage you to take the first step and stay committed to your creative journey.
- **Call to Action:** Embrace a call to action that motivates you to start making positive creative changes immediately.

NEXT STEPS:

Offer guidance on what to do after finishing the chapter to keep the momentum going. Next steps provide a clear path forward.

Examples:

- **Continued Learning:** Explore additional resources and learning opportunities to continue your creative journey.
- **Ongoing Support:** Join communities and support groups that provide ongoing motivation and guidance.

By integrating these comprehensive strategies and examples, you can craft a holistic, engaging, and practical approach to unleashing your creativity. Each element contributes to a well-rounded, effective guide that supports and inspires readers on their creative journey.

10

The Knowledge Seeker–Continuous Learning and Growth

Creativity is intelligence having fun.
—Albert Einstein

Lifelong learning, dear reader, is the elixir of perpetual growth, the magic potion that keeps our cognitive engines purring with the finesse of a well-tuned Ferrari. Imagine your brain as a super-sponge, capable of absorbing endless gallons of knowledge nectar. Each drop of wisdom you imbibe transforms you into a more enlightened, sophisticated version of yourself. Let's embark on this odyssey of intellectual adventure, delving into the manifold benefits of lifelong learning, enriched with engaging stories, theories, and examples.

1. Enhancing Cognitive Flexibility
Think of lifelong learning as yoga for your brain. Just as yoga stretches your muscles and enhances physical flexibility, continuous learning stretches your cognitive muscles, making your mind more agile and adaptable. Cognitive flexibility is the mental ability to switch between thinking about two different concepts or to think about multiple concepts simultaneously.

Example: Meet Jane, a 70-year-old retired teacher who decided to learn coding. Initially, she struggled with the syntax and logic, but over time, her brain adapted to this new way of thinking. She not only mastered coding but also found that her problem-solving skills in everyday life improved significantly.

Theory: According to the Cognitive Flexibility Theory, exposure to diverse learning experiences enhances our ability to adapt to new situations, solve complex problems, and think creatively. This theory posits that the mind, like a muscle, grows stronger with use, and continuous learning provides the exercise it needs.

2. Fostering Personal Fulfillment

Lifelong learning isn't just about accumulating knowledge; it's about enriching your life and finding personal fulfillment. The pursuit of knowledge can be a deeply satisfying endeavor, providing a sense of purpose and achievement.

Example: Consider Tom, who spent his career as an accountant but always had a passion for history. After retirement, he enrolled in history courses and even started writing a blog about historical events. This new pursuit brought him immense joy and a renewed sense of purpose.

Story: In ancient Greece, the philosopher Socrates was renowned for his quest for knowledge. Despite his wisdom, Socrates famously declared, 'I know that I know nothing,' emphasizing the importance of continuous learning and the fulfillment it brings.

3. Boosting Social Connections

Lifelong learning often involves social interactions, whether through group classes, online forums, or community workshops.

These interactions can lead to meaningful connections and a sense of belonging.

Example: Mary, a retired nurse, joined a book club to discuss her favorite novels. Not only did she enjoy stimulating conversations about literature, but she also made lifelong friends who shared her passion.

Theory: The Social Learning Theory, proposed by Albert Bandura, suggests that learning is a social activity. Engaging with others in learning activities can enhance our understanding and provide social support, which is crucial for mental well-being.

4. Improving Career Prospects

In today's fast-paced world, the job market is constantly evolving. Lifelong learning helps you stay relevant and competitive by acquiring new skills and knowledge that are in demand.

Example: John, a mid-career professional, decided to take courses in digital marketing. This new skill set not only secured his position in his company but also opened up new career opportunities he hadn't considered before.

Theory: The Human Capital Theory posits that education and training increase an individual's productivity and, consequently, their value in the job market. Continuous learning is an investment in your human capital, enhancing your employability and career growth.

5. Enhancing Mental Health

Engaging in lifelong learning can have profound benefits for mental health. It keeps the brain active, reduces the risk of cognitive decline, and can provide a sense of accomplishment and self-worth.

Example: Sarah, a retiree, took up painting classes to combat loneliness and depression. The creative process and the social interactions in her classes significantly improved her mood and overall mental health.

Story: Consider the story of Michelangelo, who, even in his later years, continued to study anatomy and improve his artistic skills. His lifelong dedication to learning kept his mind sharp and contributed to his legendary status.

6. Cultivating a Growth Mindset

Lifelong learning fosters a growth mindset—the belief that abilities and intelligence can be developed with effort and perseverance. This mindset encourages resilience and a positive attitude towards challenges.

Example: Emily, a high school student who struggled with math, adopted a growth mindset by attending extra tutoring sessions and practicing diligently. Over time, she not only improved her math skills but also developed a love for the subject.

Theory: Carol Dweck's Growth Mindset Theory emphasizes that viewing challenges as opportunities to learn and grow leads to greater success and personal development. Lifelong learners embrace this mindset, seeing every setback as a stepping stone to greater knowledge.

7. Keeping the Childlike Wonder Alive

One of the most delightful aspects of lifelong learning is that it keeps the childlike wonder alive. It's about approaching the world with curiosity, asking questions, and finding joy in discovering new things.

Example: Albert Einstein, one of the greatest minds in history, maintained a childlike curiosity throughout his life. He once said, 'I have no special talent. I am only passionately curious.' This insatiable curiosity drove his groundbreaking discoveries.

Story: Imagine a group of children on a treasure hunt, eyes sparkling with excitement as they uncover clues. Lifelong learners are like these children, always eager to explore new territories of knowledge with a sense of wonder and excitement.

8. Broadening Perspectives

Continuous learning exposes you to different viewpoints and cultures, broadening your understanding of the world. It fosters empathy and helps you see things from multiple perspectives.

Example: Alex, a corporate lawyer, decided to take a sabbatical and travel the world. He immersed himself in different cultures and took courses on international law. This experience not only broadened his legal expertise but also deepened his appreciation for diverse cultures.

Theory: The Contact Hypothesis in social psychology suggests that direct contact with different groups can reduce prejudice and foster understanding. Lifelong learning, especially through travel and cultural studies, can play a significant role in this process.

9. Encouraging Innovation and Creativity

Learning new things can spark innovation and creativity. By exposing yourself to diverse fields of knowledge, you can make unique connections and come up with original ideas.

Example: Steve Jobs, the co-founder of Apple, credited a calligraphy class he took in college for inspiring the beautiful typography on Apple computers. His willingness to explore interests outside his field led to innovative products that changed the world.

Story: Leonardo da Vinci, a quintessential lifelong learner, combined his knowledge of art, science, and engineering to create masterpieces like the Mona Lisa and innovative designs that were centuries ahead of his time. His diverse learning experiences fueled his unparalleled creativity.

10. Providing a Sense of Achievement

Finally, lifelong learning provides a sense of achievement and progress. Each new skill mastered or piece of knowledge acquired is a milestone that boosts confidence and motivation.

Example: Linda, who always dreamed of playing the piano, finally started lessons at the age of 60. Each song she learned to play filled her with pride and a sense of accomplishment, proving that it's never too late to pursue your passions.

Theory: The Self-Determination Theory suggests that the fulfillment of intrinsic goals—like personal growth and mastery—leads to greater well-being and satisfaction. Lifelong learning aligns perfectly with this theory, as it involves setting and achieving personal goals for the sake of growth and fulfillment.

THE JOYFUL JOURNEY OF LIFELONG LEARNING

Lifelong learning is not just a path to acquiring knowledge; it's a joyful journey of continuous growth and discovery. It enhances cognitive flexibility, fosters personal fulfillment, boosts social connections, improves career prospects, enhances mental health, cultivates a growth mindset, keeps the childlike wonder alive, broadens perspectives, encourages innovation and creativity, and provides a profound sense of achievement.

So, dear reader, let's embrace this journey with open minds and eager hearts. Let's be forever students, always curious, always learning, and always growing. Cheers to the joy of lifelong learning!

BUILDING A PERSONAL CURRICULUM

Creating your personal curriculum is akin to orchestrating a gourmet meal for your mind. It's a thoughtful process that requires the perfect blend of variety, substance, and delight. By curating a balanced and engaging learning experience, you can savor the joys of continuous growth. Let's delve deeper into how you can craft this intellectual feast, with points, examples, related theories, and engaging stories to guide your journey.

1. Appetizers: Light but Engaging Beginnings

Starting your learning journey with something light and engaging is essential to whet your intellectual appetite. Think of appetizers as the initial sparks that ignite your curiosity and set the stage for deeper exploration.

Example: Begin with bite-sized courses on platforms like TED Talks or Coursera. These short, engaging sessions on topics like the history of ancient civilizations or the latest scientific breakthroughs can be the perfect starters.

Story: Consider Jack, who always found history boring in school. He stumbled upon a podcast about the quirky habits of historical figures, and suddenly, history became his new passion. These fascinating tidbits opened his mind to broader historical studies.

Theory: The Primacy Effect, a principle in psychology, suggests that people tend to remember the first items in a sequence better. Starting with light and engaging content can make a lasting impression and encourage continued learning.

2. Main Course: Diving into Substantial Topics

For the main course, it's time to dive into more substantial and hearty topics. This is where the bulk of your intellectual nourishment comes from, offering depth and richness to your personal curriculum.

Example: Enroll in comprehensive courses or read in-depth books on subjects like artificial intelligence, environmental science, or classical literature. These topics provide the meat (or tofu) of your learning diet, offering a fulfilling and challenging experience.

Story: Sarah, a marketing professional, decided to learn about data analytics to enhance her career. She took a rigorous online course, which was challenging at first. However, the knowledge she gained became invaluable, transforming her career path and opening new opportunities.

Theory: Bloom's Taxonomy, a framework for categorizing educational goals, emphasizes the importance of deeper learning processes such as analyzing, evaluating, and creating. Engaging in substantial topics helps achieve higher-order thinking and meaningful understanding.

3. Side Dishes: Hobbies and Interests

Just like a gourmet meal is incomplete without delicious side dishes, your personal curriculum should include hobbies and interests that add flavor and variety to your intellectual platter.

Example: Pursue hobbies like photography, painting, or playing a musical instrument. These activities might not seem as essential as your main courses, but they provide creative outlets and enhance overall well-being.

Story: Emily, an engineer by profession, discovered a passion for pottery. This creative hobby not only provided a break from her technical work but also improved her focus and patience, positively impacting her professional life.

Theory: The Theory of Multiple Intelligences, proposed by Howard Gardner, suggests that people have different kinds of intelligences. Including hobbies and interests in your curriculum allows you to develop various intelligences, such as musical, spatial, or bodily-kinesthetic.

4. Dessert: Fun and Lighthearted Learning

For dessert, indulge in fun and lighthearted learning activities. These sweet endings keep your learning journey enjoyable and motivate you to come back for more.

Example: Watch entertaining documentaries, read graphic novels, or explore curious facts on websites like Mental Floss. These activities provide a refreshing break and keep your curiosity alive.

Story: Tom, a software developer, enjoys ending his day with episodes of a science fiction series. This lighthearted activity not only entertains him but also stimulates his imagination, leading to innovative ideas in his work.

Theory: The Hedonic Adaptation Prevention model suggests that people can maintain higher levels of happiness by introducing variety and novel experiences into their lives. Fun and lighthearted learning activities serve this purpose, ensuring your intellectual journey remains joyful.

5. Integration: Creating a Rich Tapestry of Knowledge

A well-balanced personal curriculum isn't just about cramming your brain with facts. It's about creating a rich tapestry of knowledge that makes life more delicious and fulfilling.

Example: Integrate what you learn by discussing it with others, writing about it, or teaching it. This synthesis helps solidify your knowledge and makes it more meaningful.

Story: Alex, a history buff, started a blog to share his insights on historical events. Writing about his learnings not only helped him retain information better but also connected him with a community of like-minded enthusiasts.

Theory: The Learning Pyramid, developed by the National Training Laboratories, suggests that teaching others and discussing concepts can significantly improve retention rates. Integration of knowledge through these methods enhances understanding and application.

BON APPÉTIT TO YOUR INTELLECTUAL FEAST

Crafting your personal curriculum is an art, much like preparing a gourmet meal. By thoughtfully selecting appetizers, main courses, side dishes, and desserts, you create a learning experience that is rich, varied, and deeply satisfying. Embrace this journey with curiosity and enthusiasm, and savor the delicious flavors of continuous learning. Bon appétit!

THE TREASURE TROVE OF LEARNING – UTILIZING RESOURCES FOR GROWTH

Utilizing the right resources is crucial for your intellectual growth and development. Think of resources as your magical toolkit, packed with tools to navigate the vast landscapes of knowledge. Let's explore these resources in depth, illustrating their power with points, examples, related theories, and engaging stories.

1. Books: Your Trusty Wands of Wisdom

Books are timeless treasures, each page a spell that casts wisdom and insight into your mind. They offer a deep dive into subjects, providing comprehensive knowledge and understanding.

Example: Consider the journey of Malala Yousafzai, who found solace and inspiration in books during her fight for girls' education. Her reading shaped her thoughts and fueled her determination.

Story: In Ray Bradbury's 'Fahrenheit 451,' books are banned, and a group of rebels memorize entire books to preserve their content. This story highlights the profound impact books have on preserving and sharing knowledge.

Theory: The Information Processing Theory suggests that our minds function like computers, processing the information we receive. Books provide structured, detailed information that our minds can process and retain effectively.

2. Libraries: Your Hogwarts of Knowledge

Libraries are sanctuaries of learning, offering a serene environment to explore a vast array of topics. They are hubs of curated knowledge, with resources meticulously organized for easy access.

Example: Andrew Carnegie, a steel magnate, funded the establishment of over 2,500 libraries worldwide. He believed that libraries empower individuals by providing access to knowledge and opportunities for self-improvement.

Story: The New York Public Library, with its iconic lion statues and grand reading rooms, has been a source of inspiration for countless individuals. It's where author Haruki Murakami spent hours reading and writing, shaping his literary career.

Theory: The Socio-Cultural Theory by Vygotsky emphasizes the role of social environments in learning. Libraries, as communal spaces, facilitate collaborative learning and the sharing of ideas.

3. The Internet: Your Ever-Reliable Spellbook

The internet is a limitless resource, offering a treasure trove of information at your fingertips. With online courses, tutorials, and TED Talks, you have access to the world's best professors and experts without leaving your home.

Example: Salman Khan's Khan Academy provides free, high-quality education to millions worldwide. His online platform covers a wide range of subjects, making learning accessible to all.

Story: Tim Ferriss, an author and entrepreneur, used the internet to learn new skills rapidly. His experiments with accelerated learning, documented in his books and blogs, show how the internet can be a powerful tool for personal growth.

Theory: The Connectivism Theory by George Siemens and Stephen Downes posits that learning occurs through networks and connections. The internet facilitates these networks, enabling learners to connect with diverse sources of knowledge.

4. People: Fountains of Knowledge

Human interactions are invaluable resources for learning. Engaging in conversations, asking questions, and listening to others' experiences provide unique insights and perspectives.

Example: Steve Jobs credited his success to the diverse people he interacted with. He often sought out individuals from different fields to gain fresh ideas and insights, which he then applied to his work at Apple.

Story: Socrates, the ancient Greek philosopher, used dialogues with people as his primary method of teaching and learning. His Socratic method involved asking probing questions to stimulate critical thinking and uncover underlying assumptions.

Theory: The Social Learning Theory by Albert Bandura emphasizes the importance of observing and modeling the behaviors, attitudes, and emotional reactions of others. Learning from people around us enhances our understanding and skills.

5. Travel: Injecting Curiosity Adrenaline

Traveling exposes you to new cultures, environments, and experiences, broadening your horizons and stimulating intellectual growth. It challenges your assumptions and encourages you to see the world from different perspectives.

Example: Elizabeth Gilbert, author of 'Eat, Pray, Love,' traveled to Italy, India, and Indonesia on a journey of self-discovery. Her experiences abroad led to profound personal growth and inspired millions through her writing.

Story: Mark Twain once said, 'Travel is fatal to prejudice, bigotry, and narrow-mindedness.' His extensive travels around the world greatly influenced his literary works and his understanding of human nature.

Theory: The Theory of Experiential Learning by David Kolb emphasizes learning through experience. Traveling provides immersive, hands-on learning opportunities that enrich your understanding and personal development.

6. Digital Media: Engaging and Interactive Learning

Podcasts, videos, and interactive media are modern resources that make learning engaging and accessible. They offer diverse formats to suit different learning styles, making it easier to absorb information.

Example: 'Stuff You Should Know,' a popular podcast, explores a wide range of topics in an entertaining and informative manner. Its engaging format helps listeners learn complex subjects effortlessly.

Story: The success of platforms like YouTube has democratized education. Creators like Hank Green of 'CrashCourse' produce high-quality educational videos that reach millions of viewers, making learning fun and interactive.

Theory: The Dual Coding Theory by Allan Paivio suggests that combining verbal and visual information enhances learning and memory. Digital media leverages this by providing multimedia content that reinforces understanding.

7. Mentorship: Personalized Guidance

Having a mentor provides personalized guidance and support, helping you navigate your learning journey. Mentors offer invaluable advice, share their experiences, and provide a roadmap for achieving your goals.

Example: Oprah Winfrey credits much of her success to her mentor, Maya Angelou. Angelou's wisdom and support helped Oprah overcome challenges and grow into a global icon.

Story: The relationship between Aristotle and his mentor, Plato, exemplifies the power of mentorship. Plato's teachings profoundly influenced Aristotle, who went on to become one of history's greatest philosophers.

Theory: The Zone of Proximal Development (ZPD) by Vygotsky highlights the importance of guidance in learning. Mentors help learners achieve tasks they couldn't accomplish independently, accelerating their development.

8. Nature: An Inspirational Classroom

Nature provides a tranquil environment for reflection and learning. Observing natural phenomena can inspire creativity, reduce stress, and enhance cognitive function.

Example: Charles Darwin's observations of nature during his voyage on the HMS Beagle led to his groundbreaking theory of evolution. Nature was his classroom, providing insights that changed our understanding of life.

Story: Henry David Thoreau's time spent in the woods of Walden Pond inspired his seminal work, 'Walden.' His reflections on nature and simple living continue to inspire readers to seek knowledge and meaning in the natural world.

Theory: The Biophilia Hypothesis by Edward O. Wilson suggests that humans have an innate connection to nature. Engaging with nature can enhance our well-being and stimulate intellectual growth.

9. Workshops and Seminars: Interactive Learning

Workshops and seminars offer interactive learning experiences, allowing you to engage directly with experts and peers. These events provide hands-on training and opportunities for networking.

Example: Attending a leadership workshop transformed how Priya, a mid-level manager, approached her role. The practical exercises and real-time feedback helped her develop effective leadership skills.

Story: The annual TED Conference brings together thinkers and doers from around the world. Attendees participate in workshops and seminars that spark new ideas and collaborations, showcasing the power of interactive learning.

Theory: The Constructivist Learning Theory by Jean Piaget emphasizes the importance of active involvement in the learning process. Workshops and seminars embody this by encouraging participation and hands-on learning.

FINAL THOUGHTS: EQUIP YOUR INTELLECTUAL TOOLKIT

Utilizing a diverse range of resources is key to maximizing your intellectual growth. Books, libraries, the internet, people, travel, digital media, mentorship, nature, and interactive events each offer unique benefits and opportunities for learning. By leveraging these resources, the world becomes your classroom, and every day presents a new lesson. So, equip yourself well, fellow knowledge seeker, and embark on your journey with curiosity and enthusiasm.